Dorothea Ruggles-Brise

The Delightful Pocket Companion for the German Flute

Containing a choice collection of the most celebrated Italian, English, and Scotch

tunes. Vol. 2

Dorothea Ruggles-Brise

The Delightful Pocket Companion for the German Flute
Containing a choice collection of the most celebrated Italian, English, and Scotch tunes. Vol. 2

ISBN/EAN: 9783337410971

Printed in Europe, USA, Canada, Australia, Japan

Cover: Foto ©Thomas Meinert / pixelio.de

More available books at **www.hansebooks.com**

THE DELIGHTFUL

Pocket Companion.

For the

GERMAN FLUTE

Containing

A Choice Collection of the most Celebrated Italian, English, and Scotch Tunes, Curiously Adapted to that Instrument.

LONDON,

Printed for R: BREMNER, *opposite Somerset House*

in the STRAND.

Where may be had. Variety of new Music for all Instruments

Balmy Sweetness. By Mr. Boyce.

Vol 2d Part 1st

Musette. By Mr Howard.

Minuet

The Wood Cutters

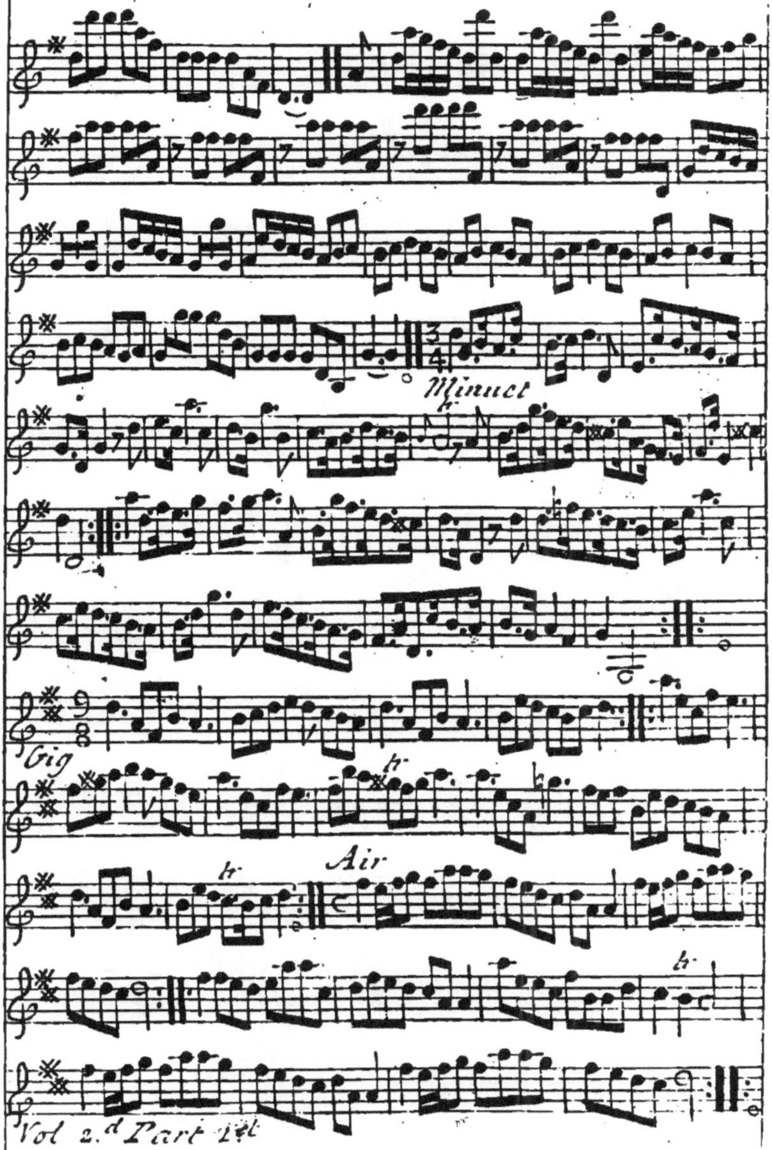
Minuet
Gig
Air
tr

The Chace is o'er. By Mr. Howard.

Minuet by Sig.r Hasse

Minuet

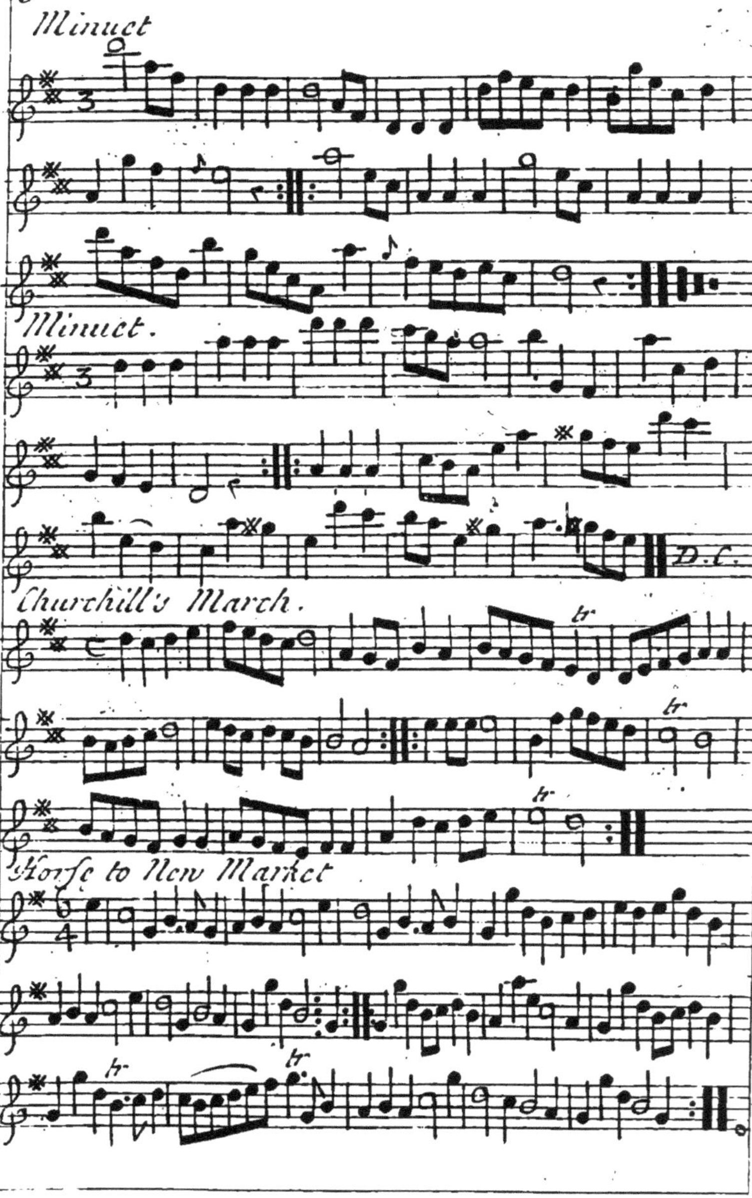
Minuet
Minuet.
D.C.
Churchill's March.
tr
Horſe to New Market
tr

A Favourite Minuet

Minuet

Come bid adieu to Fear. By Mr. Arne.

Con Spirito

Vol 2d Part 1st

A Favourite Air

And⁰

Minuet

Minuet

Ravenscroft's Fancy

Vol 2d. Part 1st

Auretti's Dutch Skipper Dance

Presto

Allo

The Ridotta

Presto

Minuet

Gig

March. Danc'd in the Hay Makers by Sig.r Boromeo.

Minuet, in the Thunder & Lightning Dance.

Danc'd by M.dm Bonneval.

Come and trip it

Air by Mr. Handel

Il Ritornel Da Capo

Vol 2d Part 1st

24

Minuet

The Inconstant

Bell Size

Air by Mr Hudson

In Praise of Burgundy

Vol 2d Part 1st

Minuet

Larghetto

Jack the Horse Courser.

Harlequin Hermit.

Fox Hunters Jigg.

Tell me lovely Shepherd. By Mr Boyce.

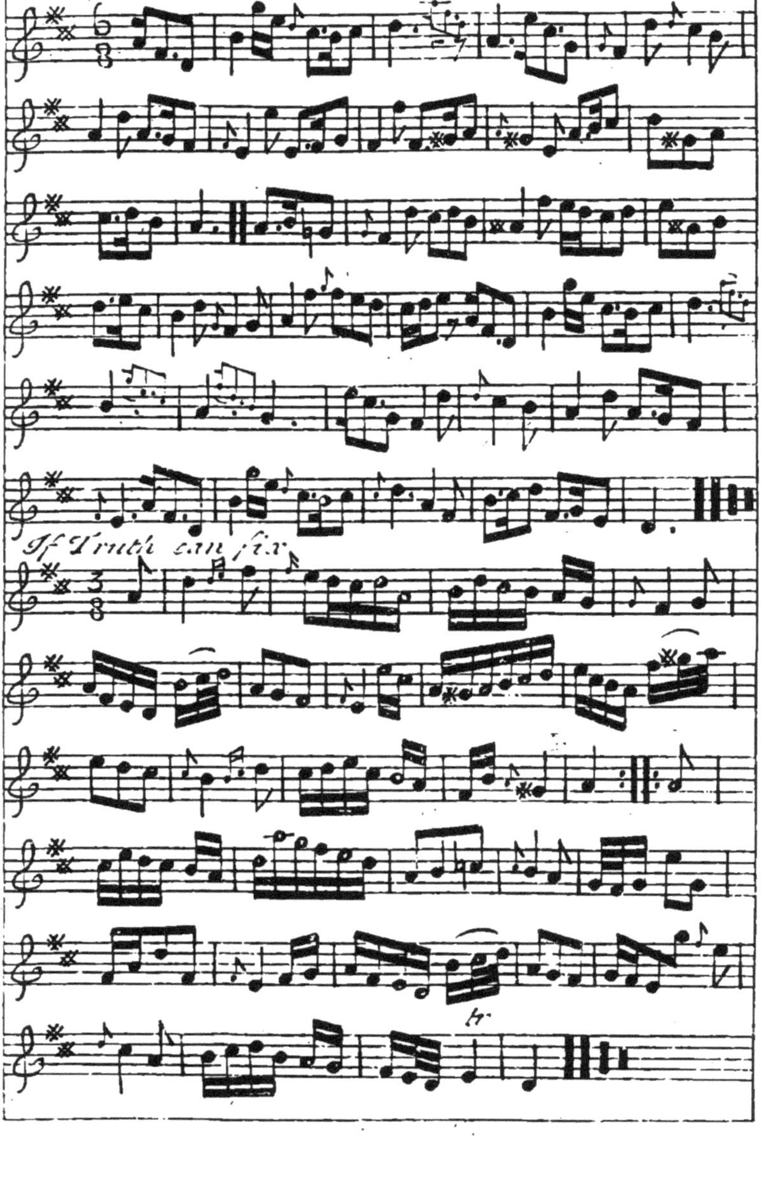
If Truth can fix
tr

By dimpled Brook. By Mr. Arne.

Ande

Pig in the Parlour

Good Mother

Vol 2d Part 1st

Ye Virgin Pow'rs By Mr. Howard.

The new flown Birds By Mr. Lampe.

Andantino

Is there a Charm. By Mr. Carey.

Twas in the Bloom of May. By Mr. Howard.

Harlequin Shipwreck'd.

Crowns of sweet Roses. By Mr. Handel.

Too plain dear Youth

Hornpipe by Mr. Handel.

Pere

Glover's Grecian Dance.

Drunken Peasant

A Trip to the Laundry

Vol 2.d Part 1.st

24

King's Arms

By the gayly circling Glass

All alive and merry.

Now Phœbus sinketh. By Mr. Arne.

Vol 2d Part 1st

Minuet in Tamerlane. By Mr. Handel.

Larghetto

Fausan's Minuets

End with the first Minuet.

Air by Mr. Boyce.

Alló ma non troppo

At setting Day. By Mr. Hoyard.

Lively but not too fast.

Vol 2d. Part 1st.

28

Air by Mr Boyce.

Air by M.ͬ Howard.

Air by M.ͬ Howard.

Air by M.ͬ Howard.

30

The fond Shepherdess. By Mr. Galliard.

Had Neptune. By Mr. Powell.

Air by Mr Boyce

Come little Cupid.

Miller of Mansfield.

Vol. 2d. Part 1st

Air by Mr. Howard

Air by Mr. Howard

Air by Mr. Howard.

L'amo tanto. By Sig.r Attilio.

D.C

Running Footman

Vol 2d Part 1st

Allegro in Pastor fido. By Mr. Handel.

Minuet

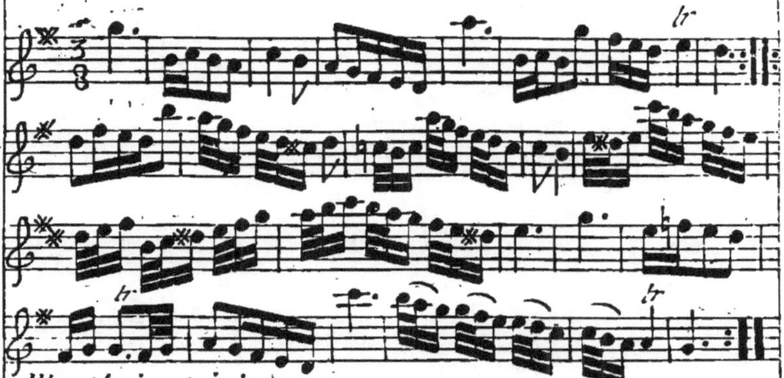

March in Scipio

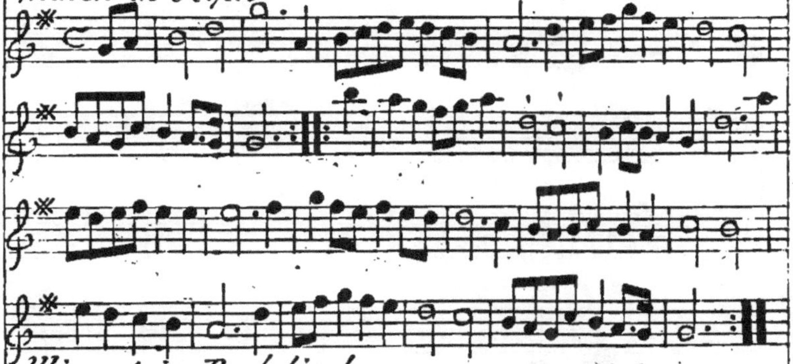

Minuet in Rodelinda.

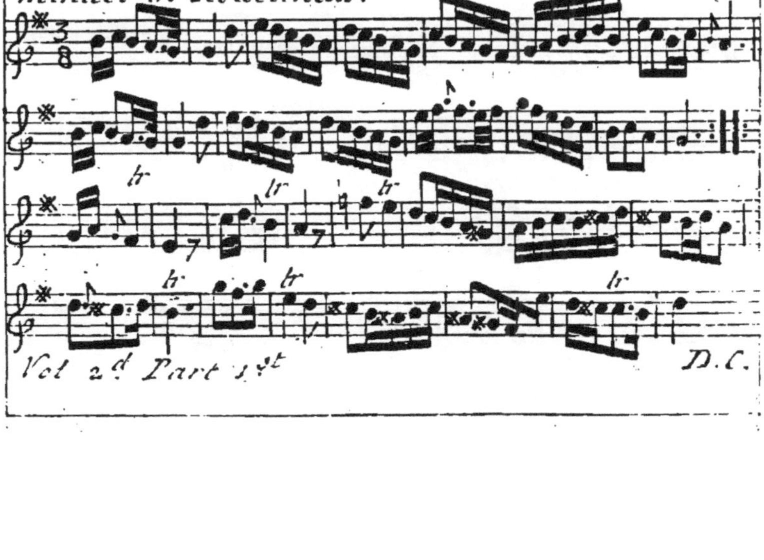

D.C.

Allegro in Scipio By Mr Handel

When Love and Youth

The Hounds are all out.

The following Airs by Mr Snow.

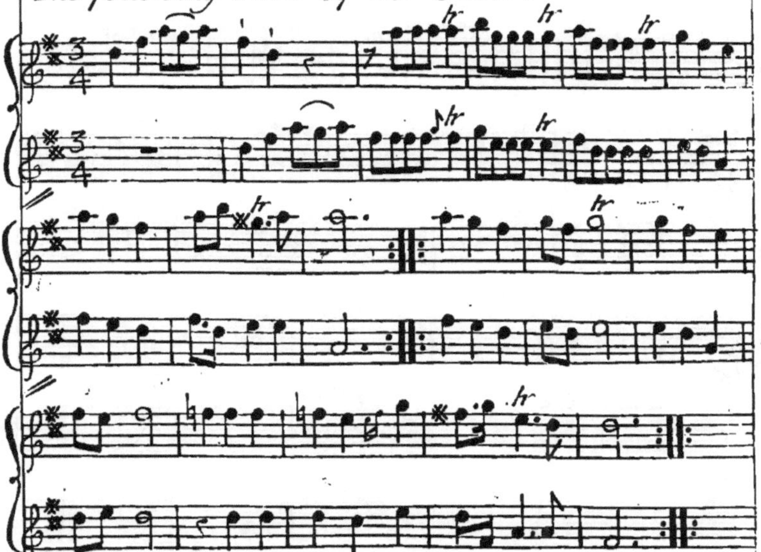

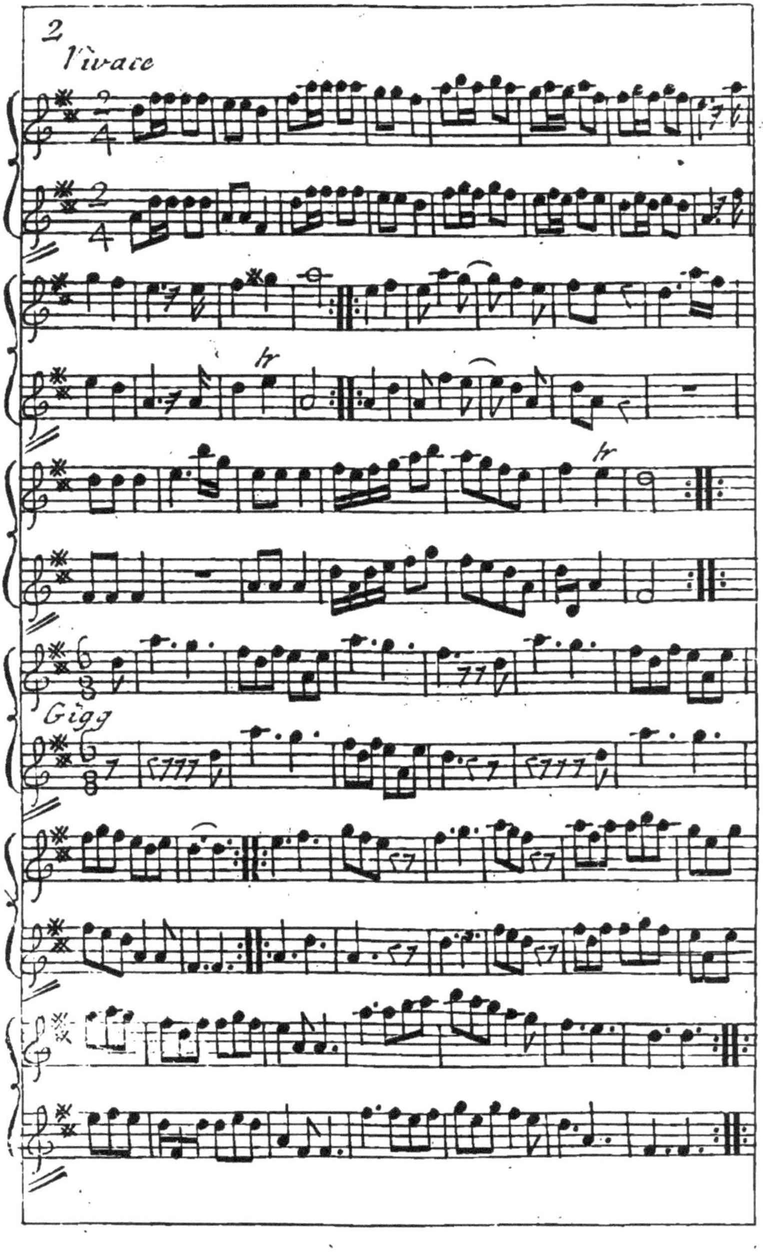
2
Vivace
tr
tr
Gigg

Allegro

Adagio

Vol 2.d Part 2.d

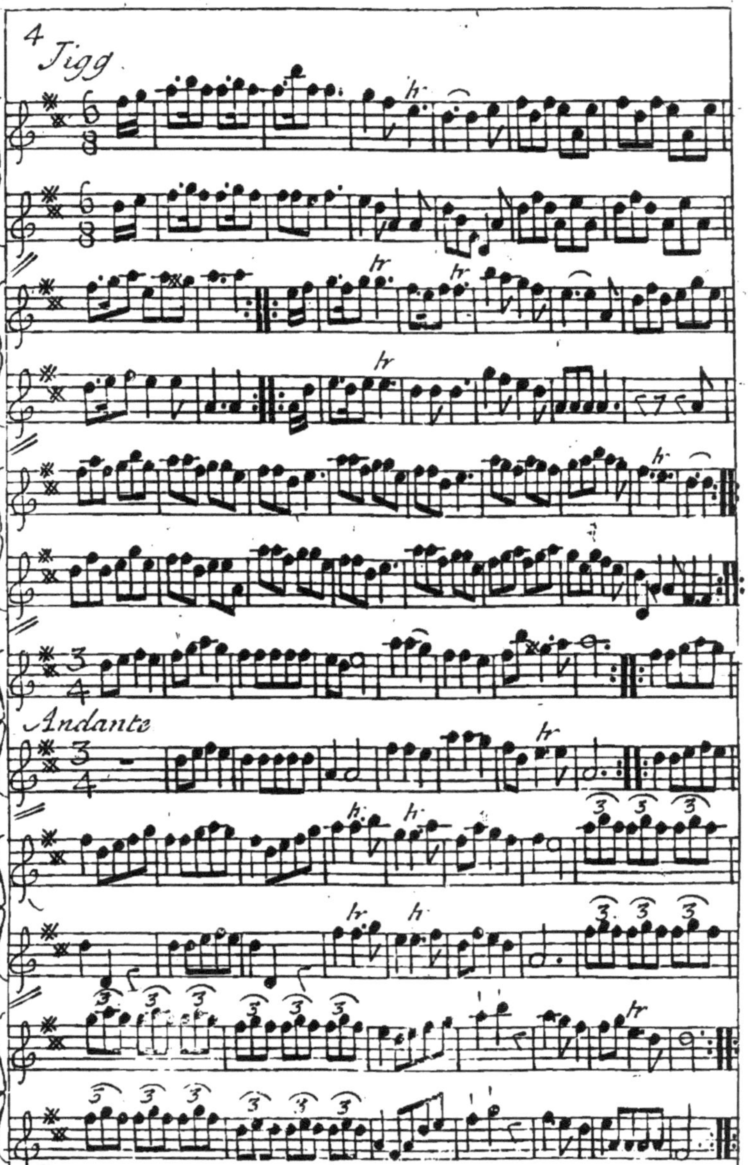
Jigg
Andante

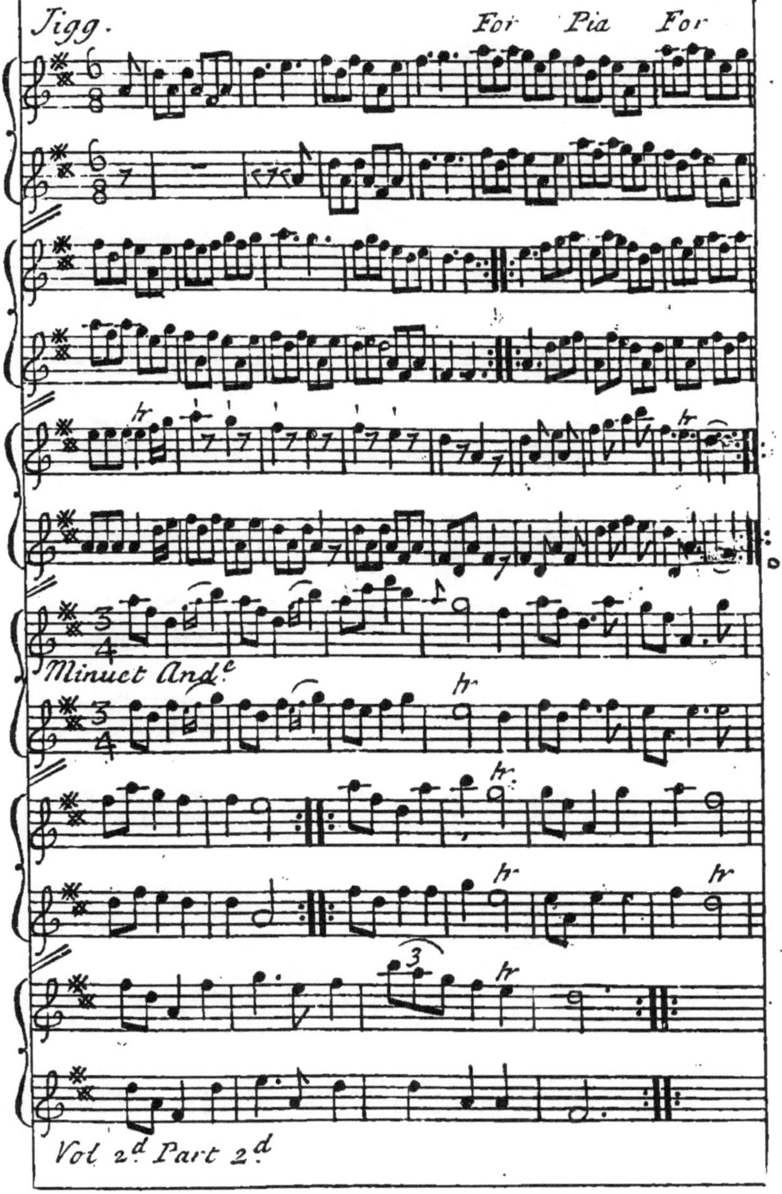
Jigg.
For Pia For
Minuet And^e

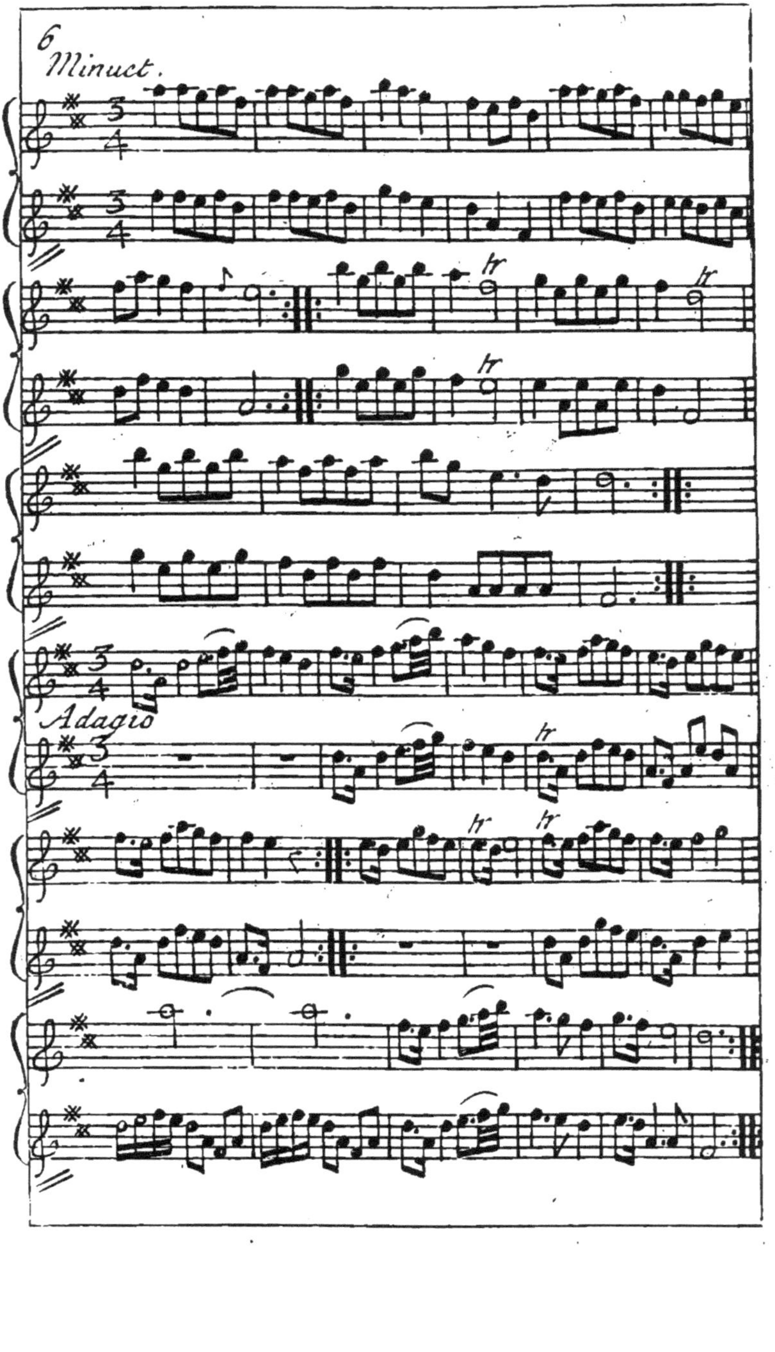
6
Minuet.
Adagio

Minuet

Da Capo

Minuet Al

8

The following Airs by Mr. Messing.

Largo assai

ad libitum

Minuet

Vol 2ᵈ Part 2ᵈ

10

Andante

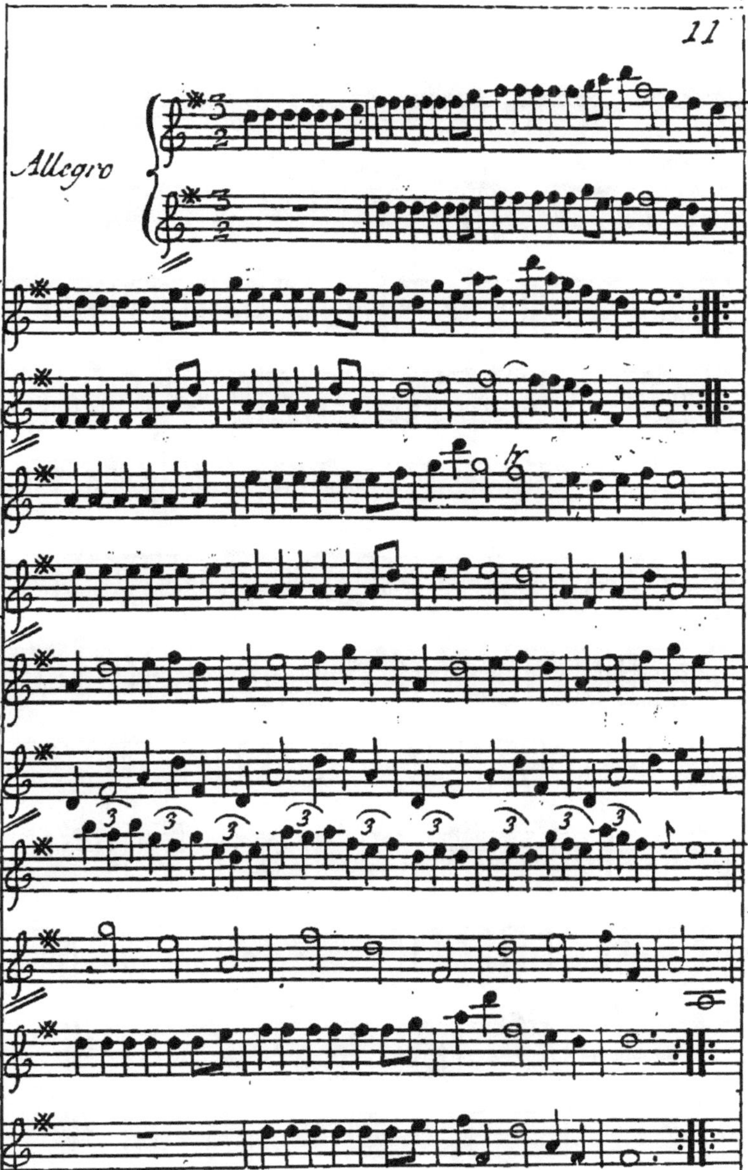
Allegro
Vol 2d Part 2d

Minuet

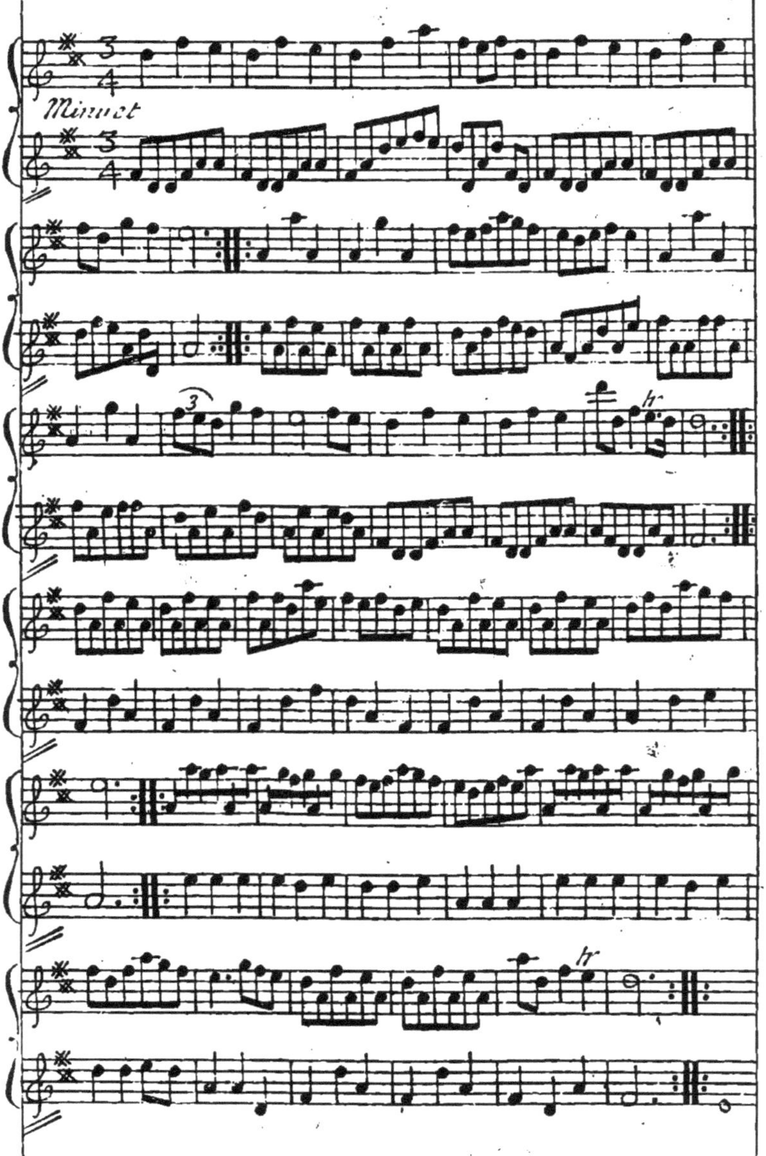

Adagio

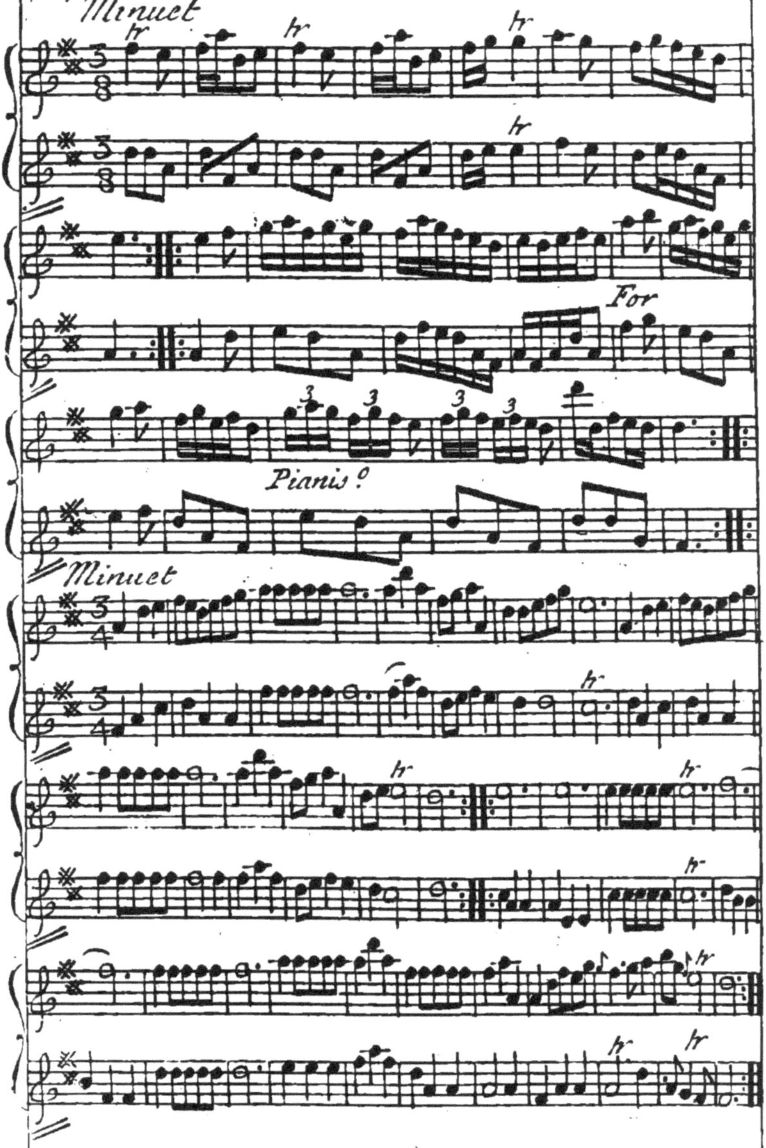
Minuet
tr
For
Pianis:
Minuet

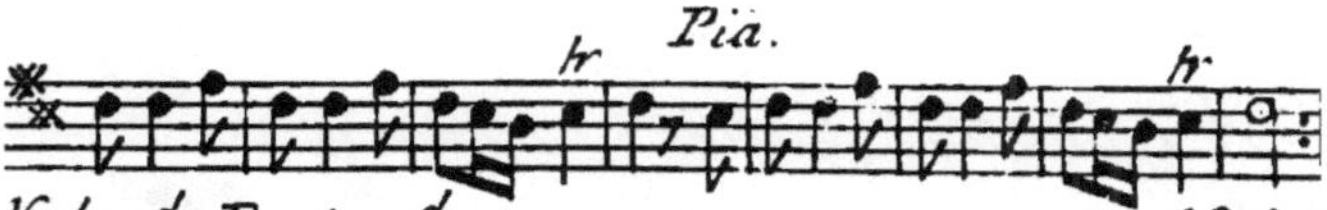

Vol 2.d Part 2.d *Volti*

16 *Air by sig.r Vinci*

Allegro

Minuet by Sigr. Vinci.

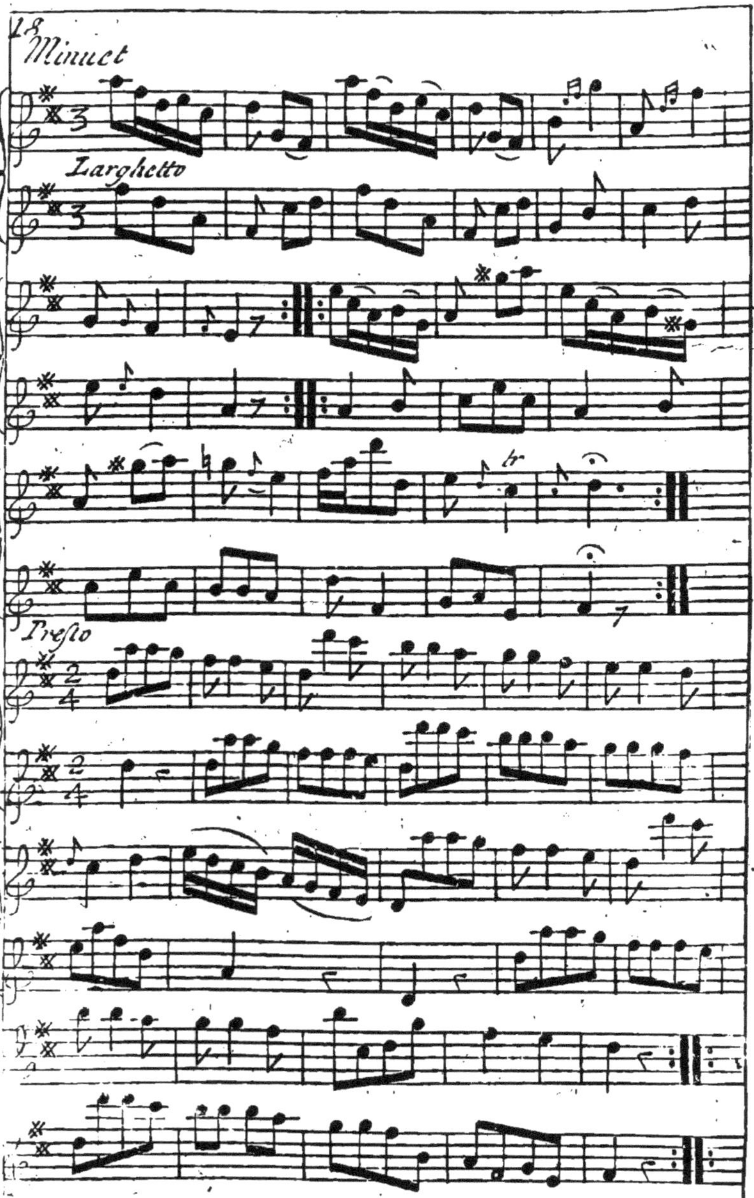
Minuet
Larghetto
tr
Preſto

Minuet Da Capo

A Trumpet March

A French Horn March.

Minuet

Minuet by Sigr Vinci.

French Horn Minuet

Vol 2.ᵈ Part 2.ᵈ

French Horn Minuet.

The following Airs by Mr. Oswald.

Andante

The Redota Minuet

Vivace

26

Air

Andante

Minuet

Vol 2ᵈ Part 2ᵈ

Siciliano

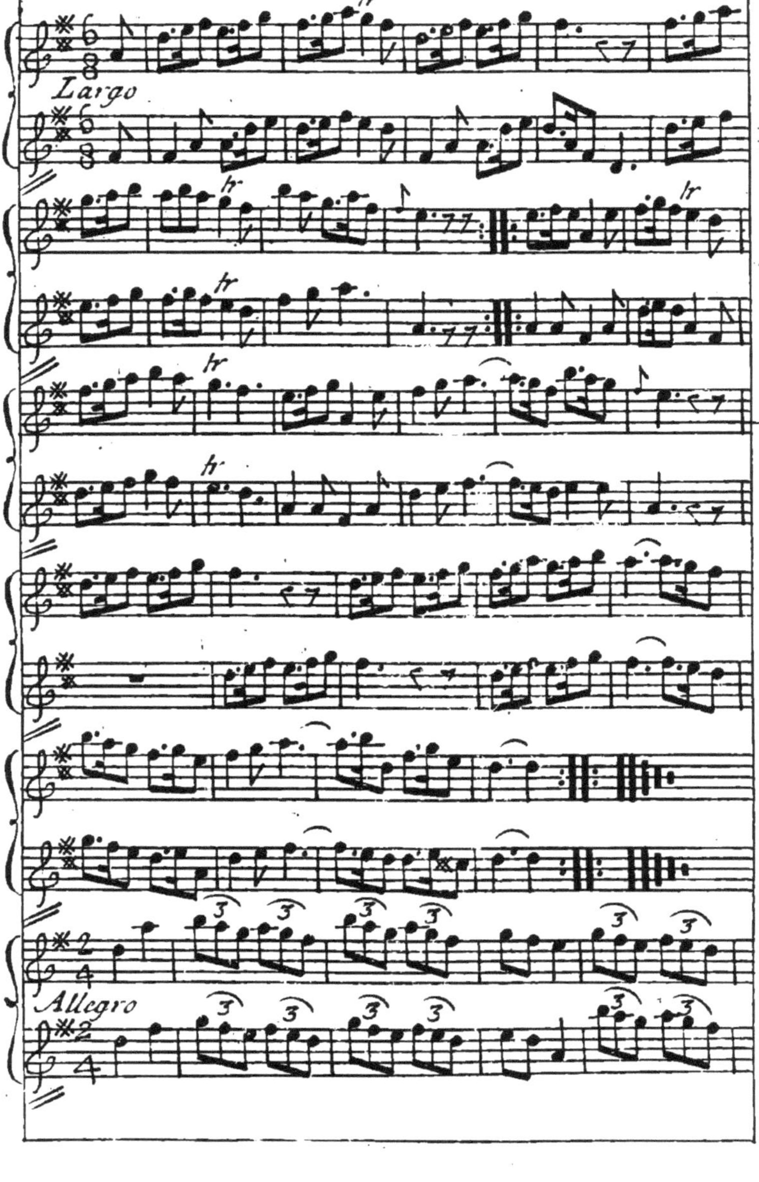

Gavotta

Vivace

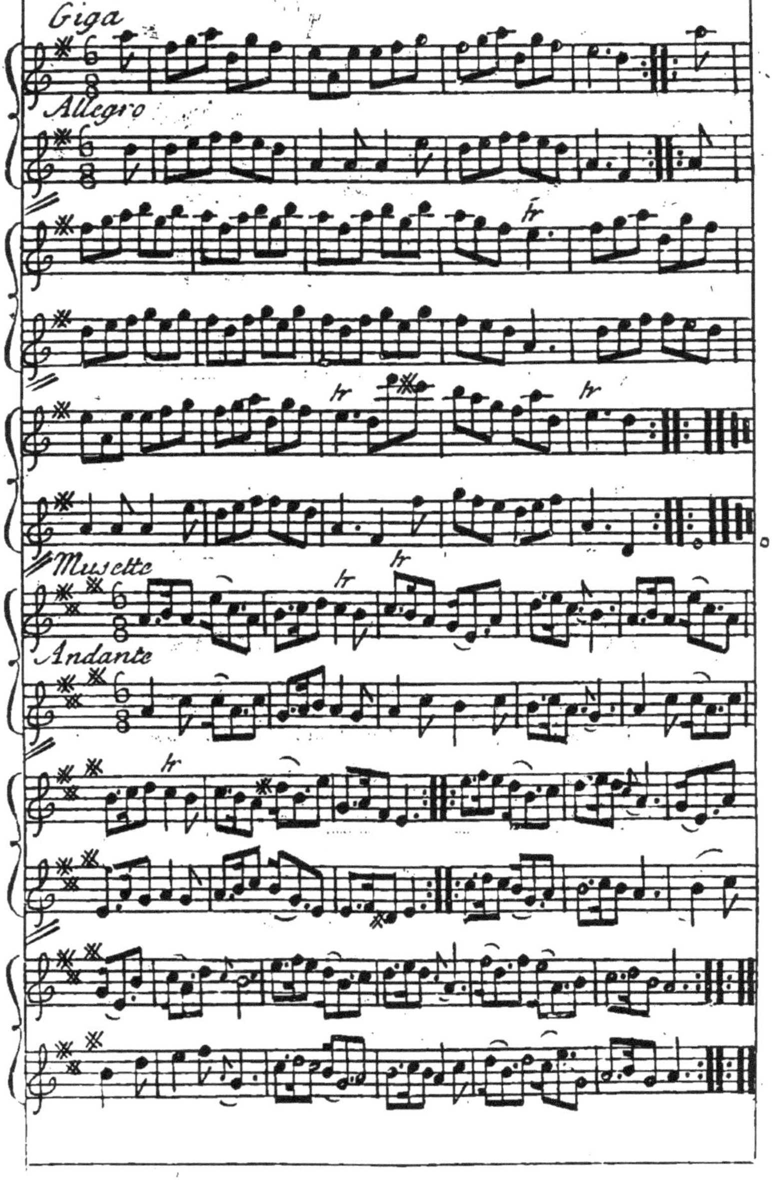
Giga
Allegro
Musette
Andante

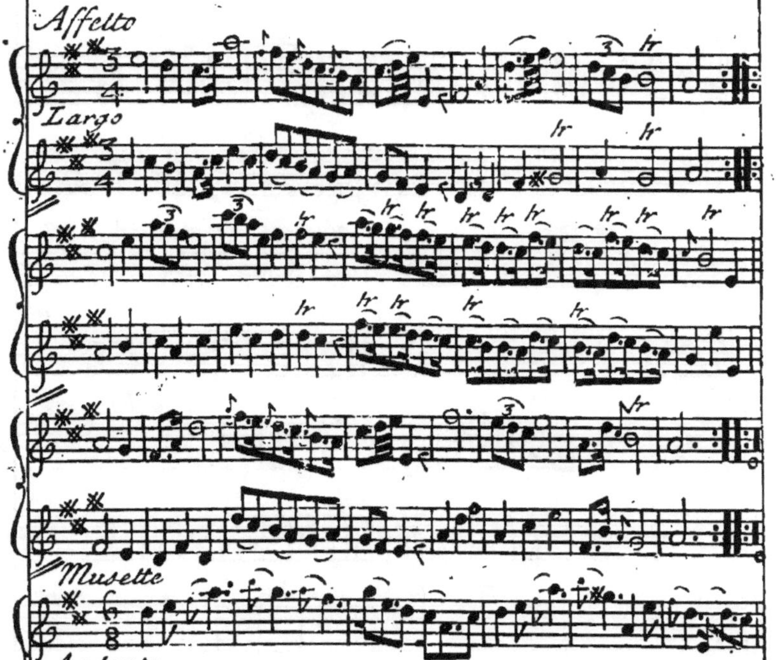
Affetto
Largo
Musette
Andante

Minuet

Vivace

Andante

34 Aria

A March

Allegro

Musette

Largo Andante

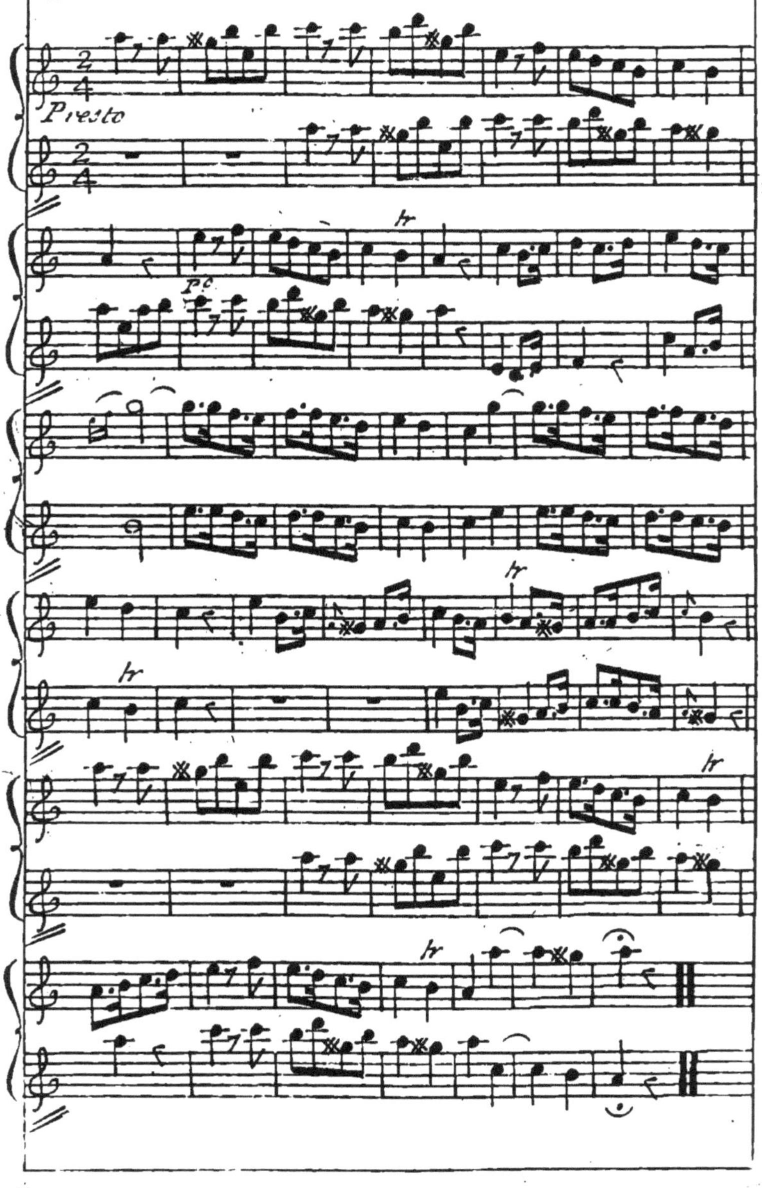
Presto
p.e
tr

Phillis and Silvano. By Mr. Festing.

Ask me not how calmly I.

Vol 2ᵈ Part 3ᵈ

Minuet by Sigr. St. Martini.
Nº 1.
Rondo
Fine
Nº 2.
Da Capo Nº 1

Gentle Love. By Comte de St. Germain.

Vol 2d Part 3d

The Judicious fair One. By Mr. Holcombe.

Air by Mr Oswald.

Air by Mr Lampe.

6

Air by Comte de St Germain.

The Constant Lover. By Mr Boyce.

A Favourite Air by Mr Chilcot.

Balin a mong.

End with the first Symphony

Vol 2.^d Part 3.^d

8

Minuet by Mr. Granom.

Variation

Hark hark o'er the Plains

Air by Mr Burges
Andᵗᵉ

A Favourite Air by Mr. Hodson.

Moggy's Complaint. A favourite Air.

12
Air by Mr. Hornik.

Minuet

Minuet by Mr Pescetti

Auretti's Minuet.

2d Minuet

Minuet by Mr Granom.

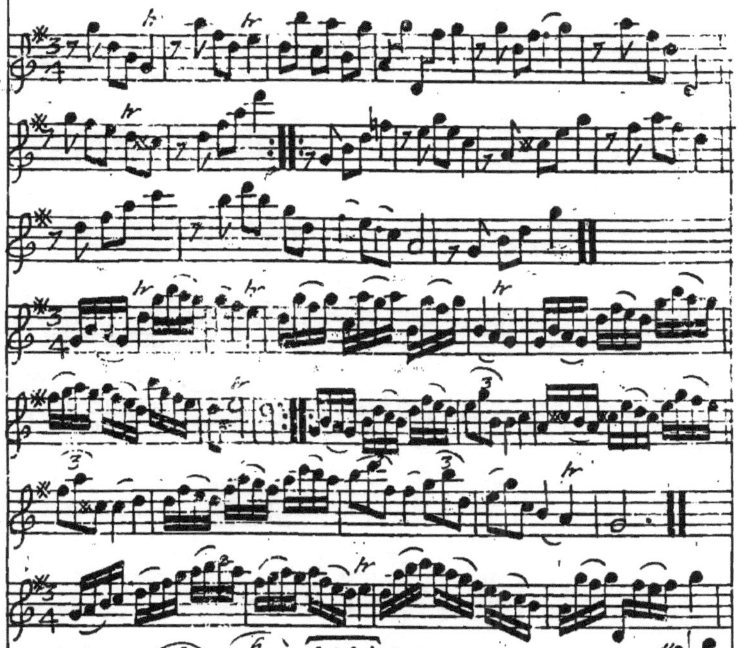

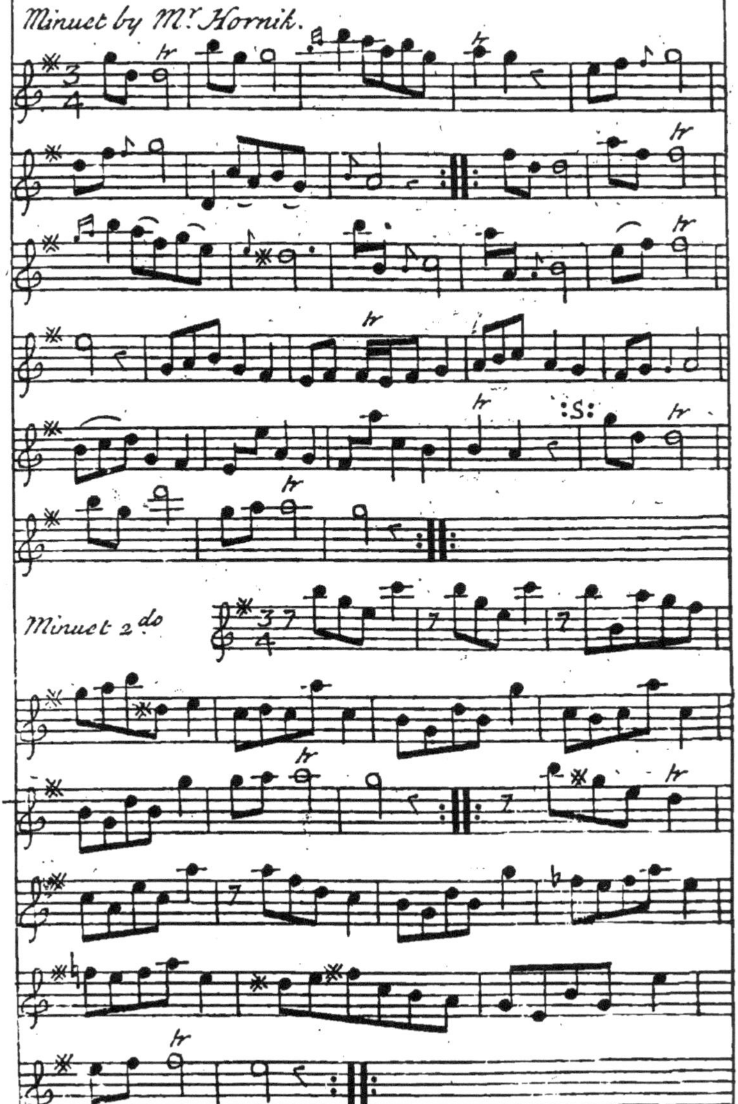
Minuet by Mr. Hornik.
Minuet 2do
Minuet 1mo Da Capo

By Jove I'll be free. By Mr Boyce.

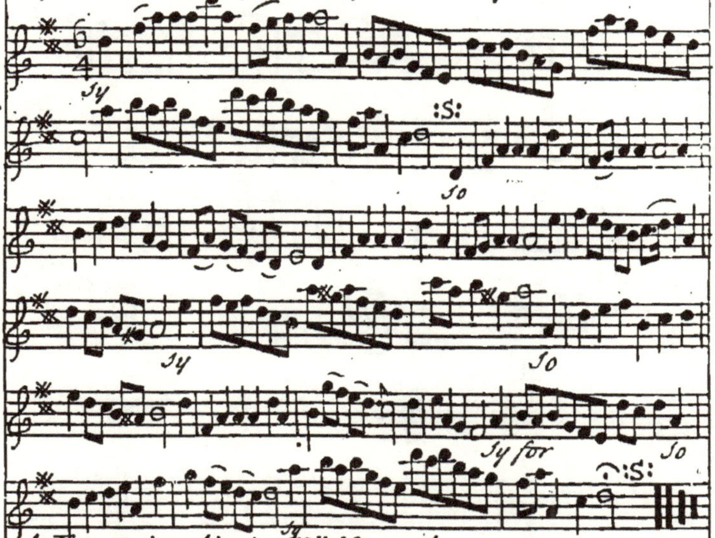

A Favourite Air by Mr Howard.

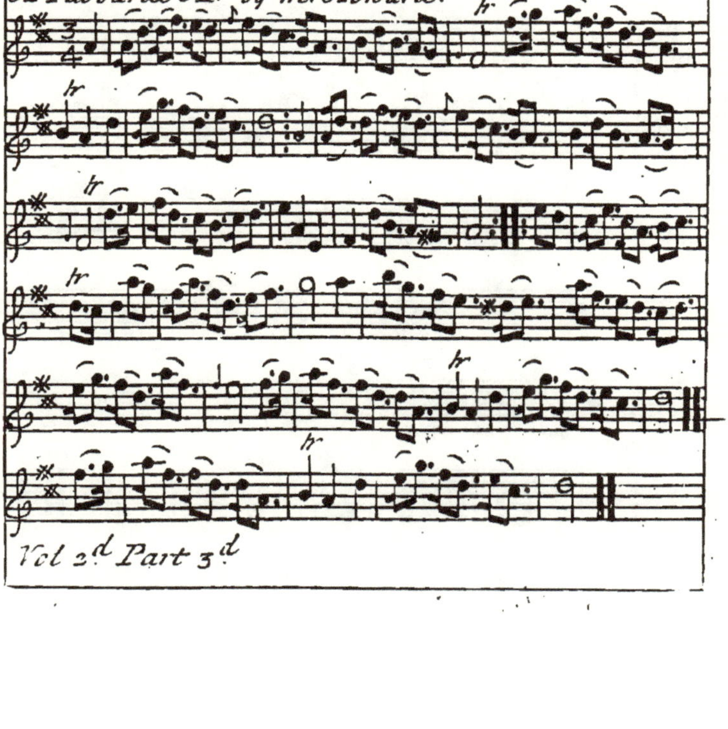

18

Minuet by M.ᵣ Granom.

A Favourite Air by Mr. Chilcot.

A Favourite Air by Mr. Oswald.

Vol 2d Part 3d

A Favourite Air by Comte de St Germain.

A Favourite Air by Mr Handel.

Chorus

Pia

For

Minuet by Mr Granom.

Minuet by Sigr. St. Martini.

Vol 2.ᵈ Part 3.ᵈ

Minuet by Mr Hornik

Minuet 2do

Minuet 1mo Da Capo

The Choice. By Mr. Holcombe

Air by Sigr. F.E.S.

Minuet by Mr. Granom.

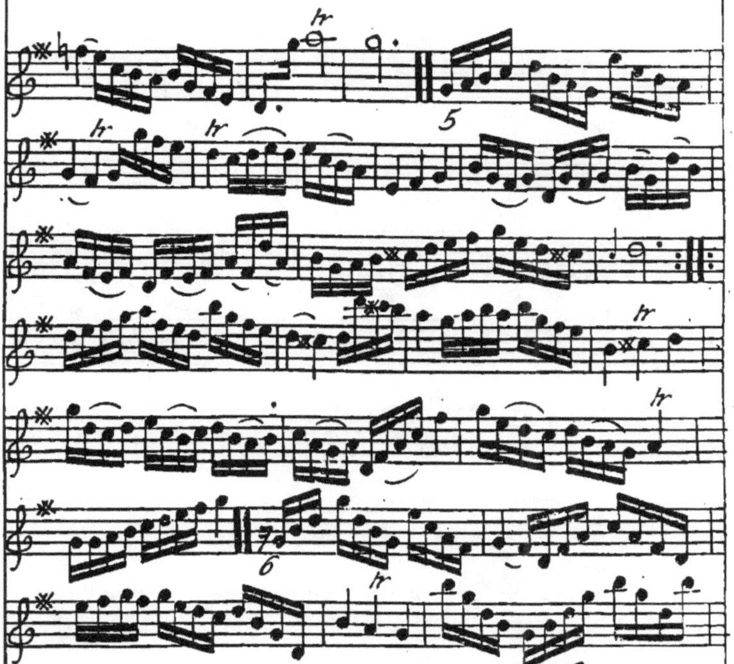

Minuet by Sigr. St. Martini.

2d. Minuet

Da Capo al Primo Minuetto per Fine.

The Jene scay quoi. Set by Mr Handel.

A favourite Air by Mr Worgan.

Vol 2d Part 3d

Air by Mr Granom.

Presto

Jigg.

The fair Thief. by Mr Worgan.

A favourite Air by Mr Crookenden.

Vol 2d Part 3d

A favourite Air by Mr Oswald.

A favourite Air by Mr Boyce.

A Favourite Air by Mr. Corfe.

A Favourite Air in the Foundling.

34

Air by Dr Green.

Jigg by Mr Granom

Silvia. A Favourite Air.

A Favourite Air by Mr. Worgan.

A Favourite Air by Mr. Defesch.

Dione. By Mr Arne.

The Caution By Mr Arne.

Vol 2d Part 4th

Collin and Phœbe. By Mr. Arne.

Chorus for three German Flutes.

Phillis. By Mr. Arne.

Andt Sy.

Pia

For

Blow ye bleak Winds. By Mr Arne

Allegrissimo

Yes I'm in Love. By Mr Arne

Love and Wine. By Mr. Arne.

6

Behold the sweet Flow'rs. By Mr. Arne.

Sym. 2ᵈ Time Fortißimo.

My roving Heart. By Mr. Arne.

Damon and Cloe. By Mr. Arne.

The Hungarian March.

When Isicles . By Mr. Arne .
Sy
tr
Poco All.o
:S:
So
Sy
So
Sy
:S:
So
Sy
So
Imitate the Owl.
Lord Cathcart's or Bath Minuet.
tr
3
Vol 2d Part 4th

Thamis Nysa. By Mr. Arne.

Allegro non troppo

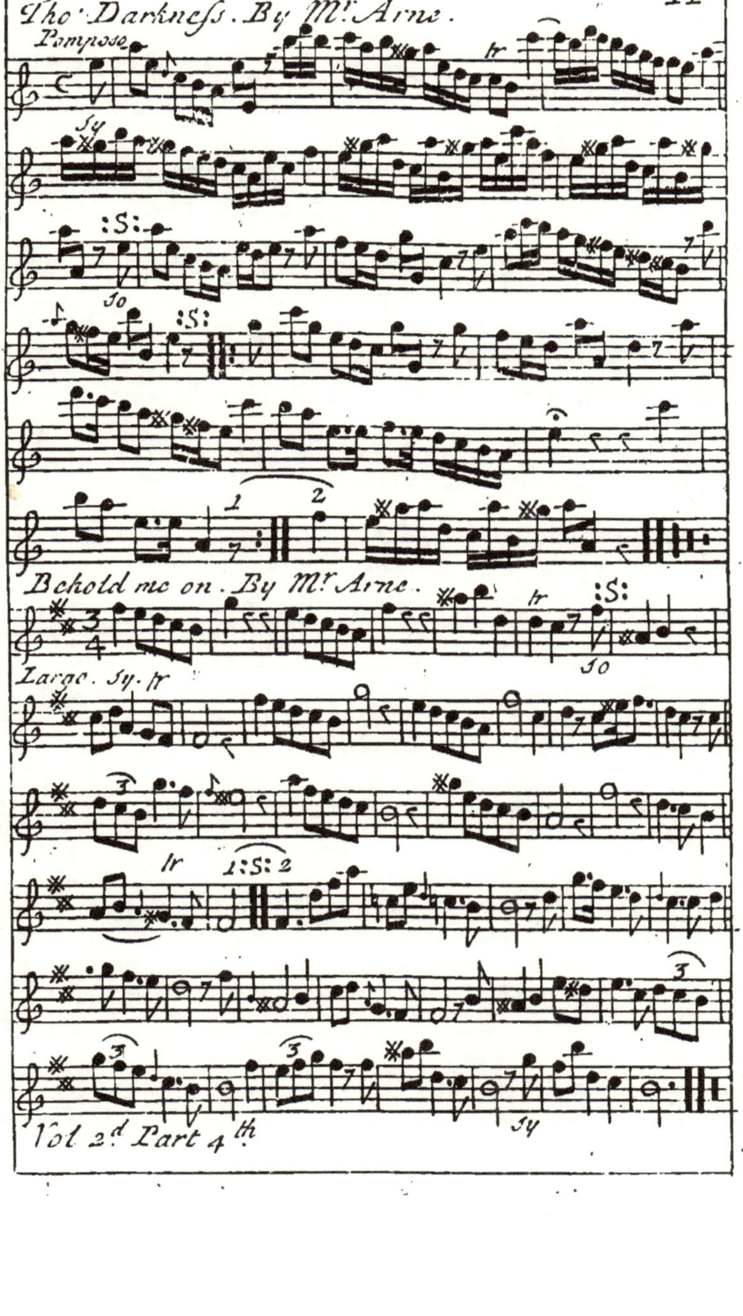
Tho' Darkness . By Mr. Arne .
Pomposo
Behold me on . By Mr. Arne .
Largo .

As Death alone. By Mr. Arne.

Silvia wilt thou. By Mr. Arne.

Andantino

The Boy thus. By Mr. Arne.

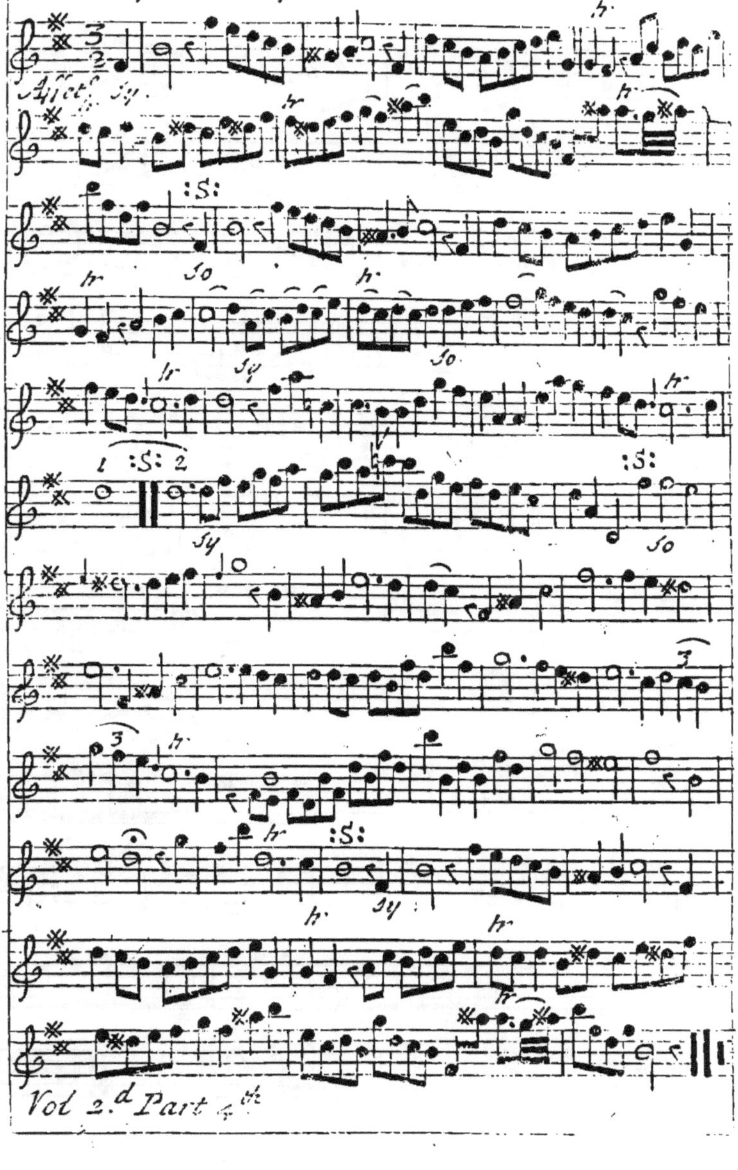

14
Dear Cloe. By Mr. Arne

Not too fast.

Foot's Minuet.

To keep my gentle Jessy. By Mr Arne.

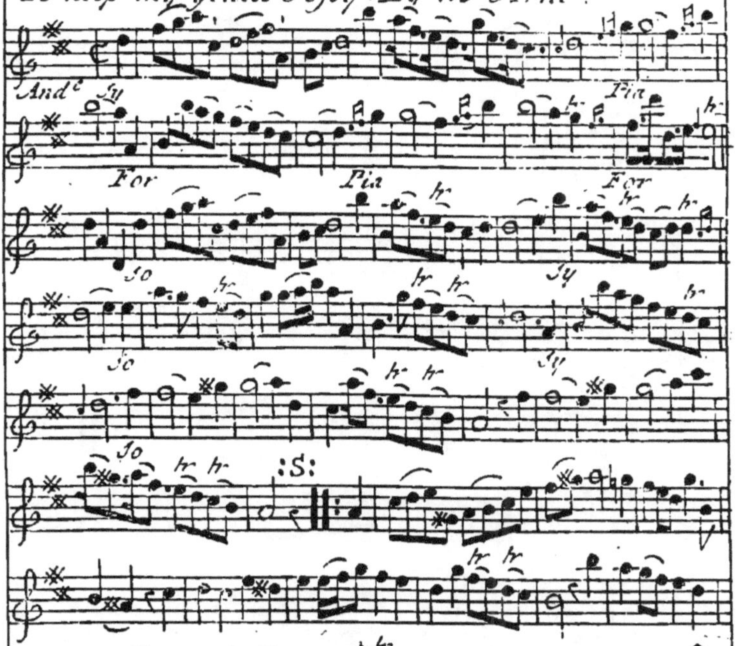

Observe the fragrant. By Mr. Arne.

My Bliss too long. By Mr. Arne.

A Favourite Duett by Mr Arne.

17

Non troppo Allo.

Vol 2d Part 4th

Volti

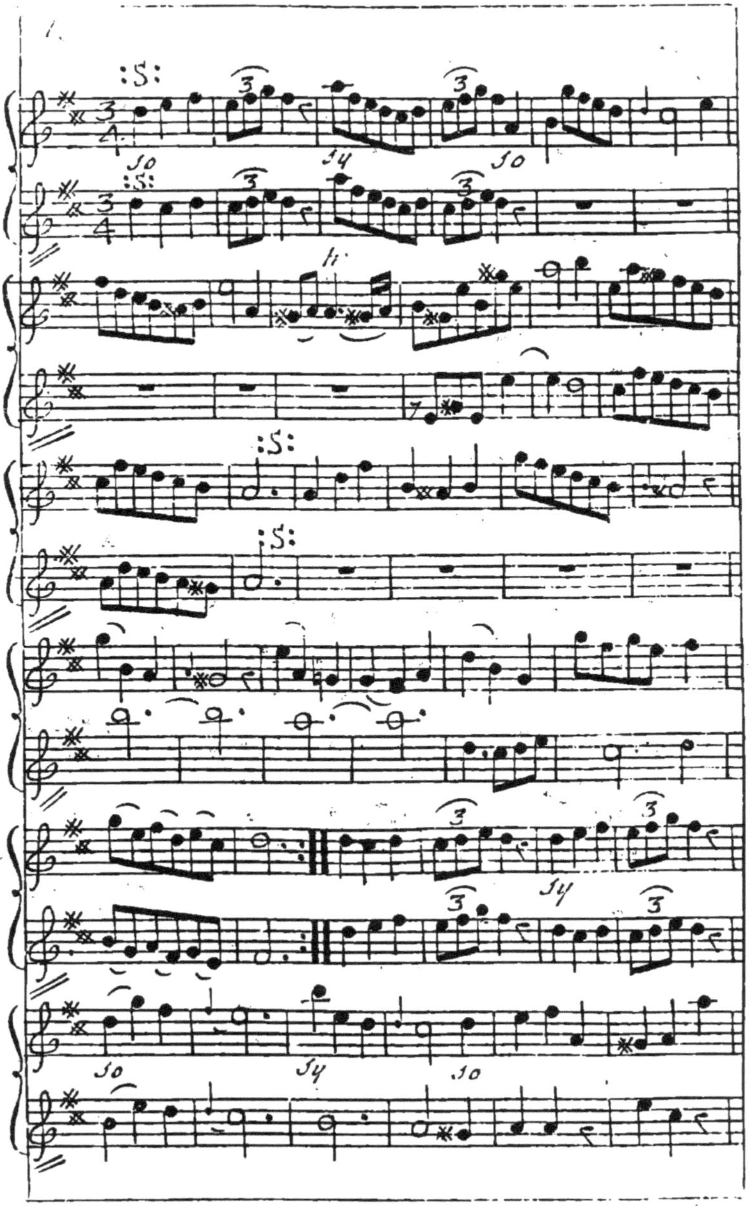

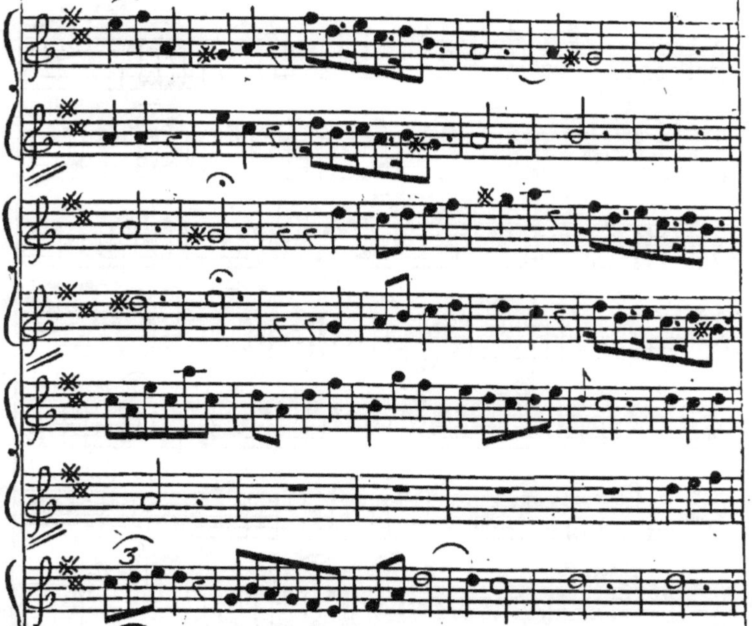
Sy

When gentle Parthenissa. By Mr Arne

Blow. blow. By Mr Arne.

Minuet by Mr Handel.

Isabel by Mr Arne.

Vol 2d Part 4th

Minuet by Sig.r Carporale.

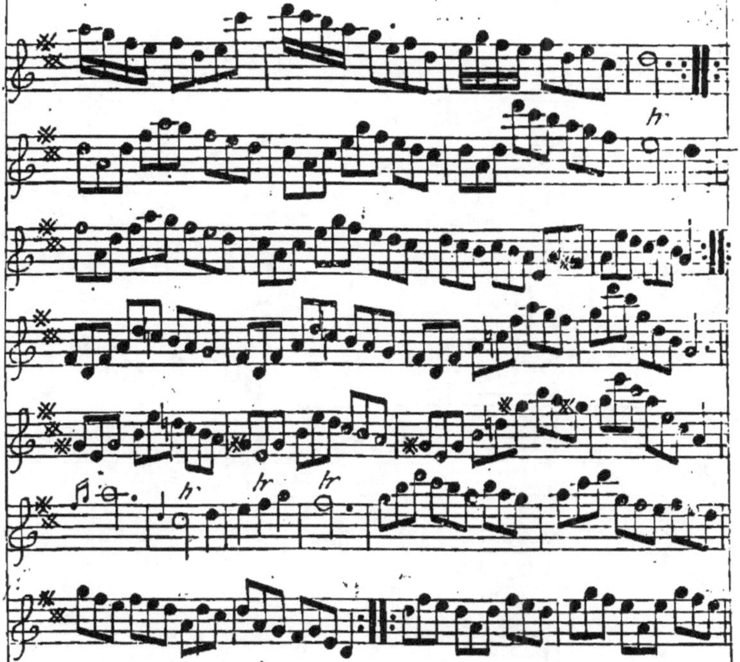

Come Rosalind. By Mr. Arne.

Gavot by Mr Granom

Vol 2d Part 4th

Charming Delia By Mr. Crookenden.

Duett By Sigr Carlo Wiseman

Spiritoso

Vol 2d Part 4th

Trumpet Tune.

March.

Prince William's March

Gavot by Corelli.

A Favourite Gavot

The following Minuets by Mr. James Stolger.

Minuet

Minuet

Minuet

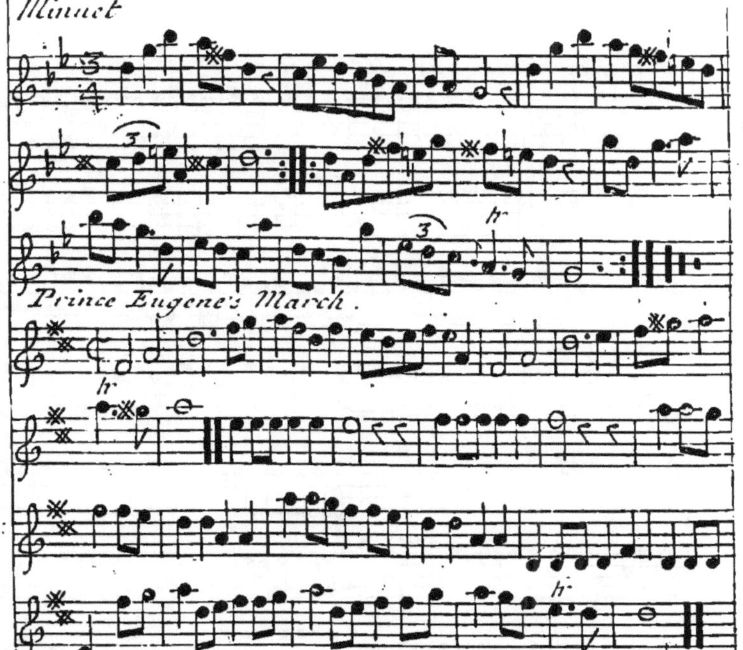
Minuet
Prince Eugene's March.
Winfield's March.

32

Trumpet Minuet by Mr. Grano

New Foot Guards March

Gen's Arms March.

Minuet

Rigadoon

D.C.

Air

Staccato

Vol 2ᵈ Part 4ᵗʰ

Allmanda by Corelli

Gavot by Do

Air

Air

Minuet

Duke of Ormond's March.

Marlborough's March.

Vol 2.d Part 4.th

Minuet by Mr. Granom.

Gavot

Gentle Youth O tell me why. By Mr. Arne.

Largo.

Young Delia &c. By Mr. Arne.

A Tempo di Gavotta

Vol. 2d Part 5th

1

A Maiden's soft Wailings. By Mr Arne.

Andante. Largo e amoroso

At length too soon &c. By Mr Arne.

Andᵉ

The gentle budding Rose behold.

Minuet by Mr. Petzold.

Moderato

A Duett by Mr. Broderip

Check the growing Idle Passion.

4

But had the Shepherd

Andante

Adieu Edina friendly Seat.

Affettuoso!

Minuet by Mr. Petzold.

Andᵗᵉ

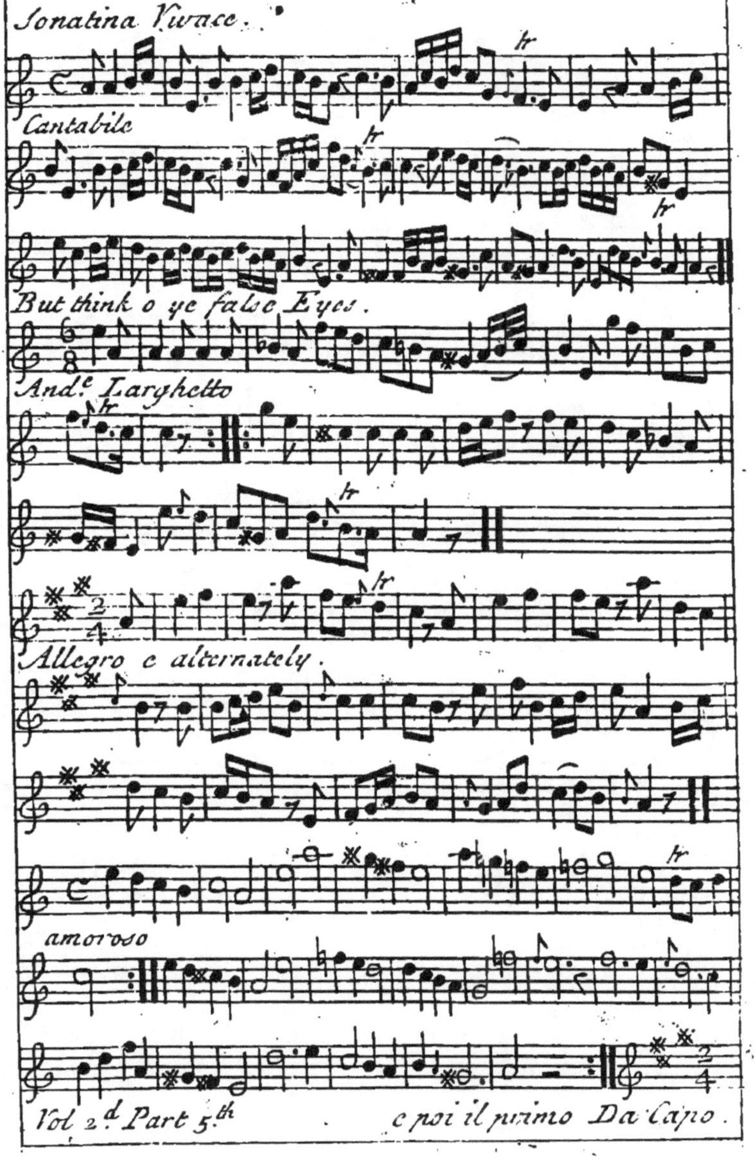

e poi il primo Da Capo.

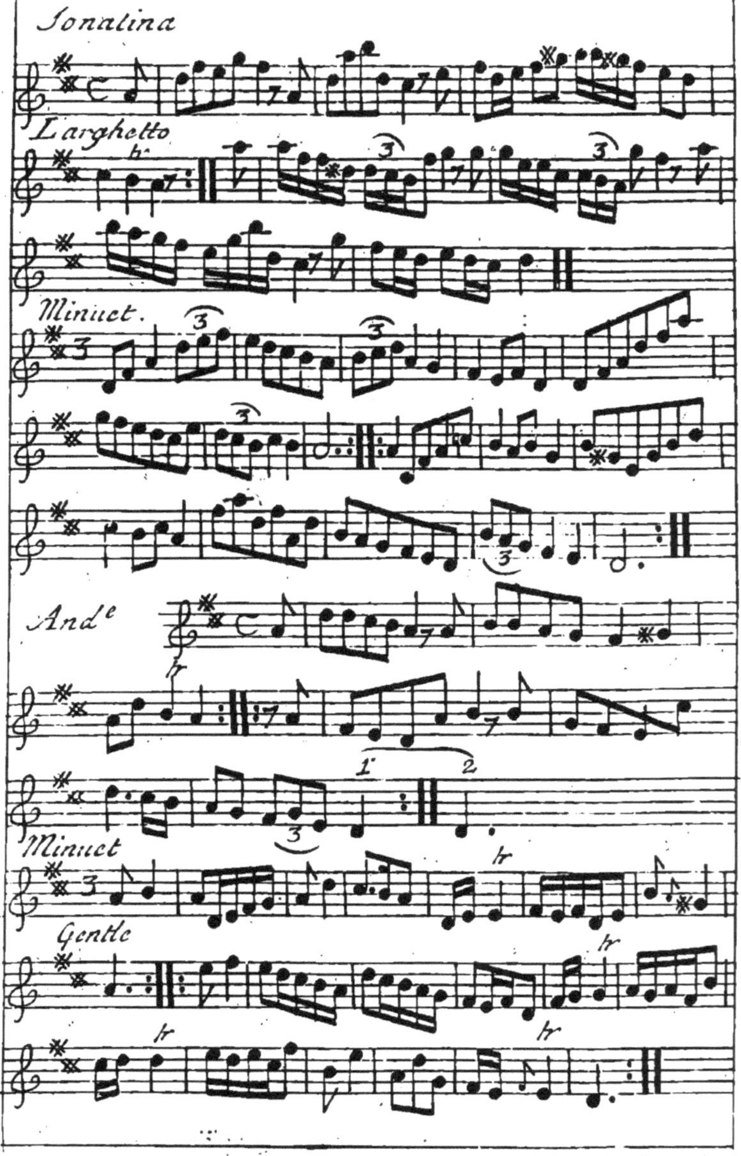
Sonatina
Larghetto
Minuet.
Andᵉ
Minuet
Gentle

Sonata in a Scotch Taste.

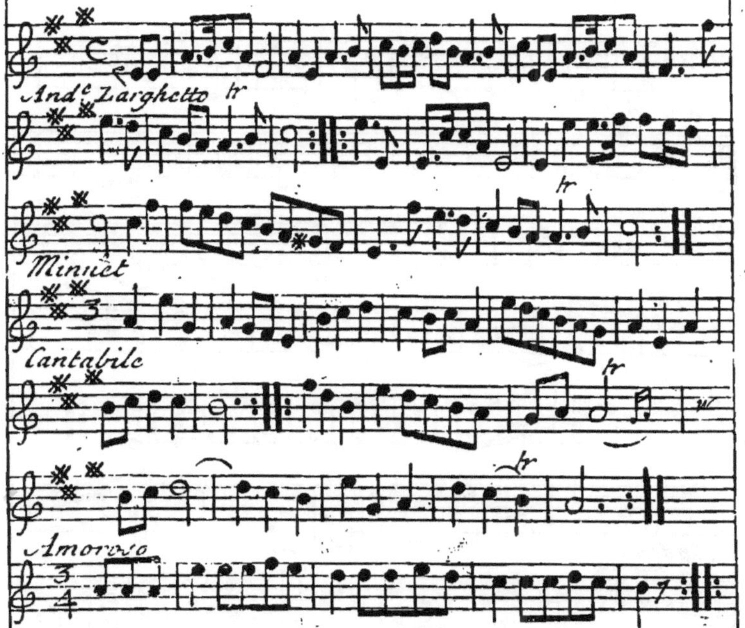

Sonata

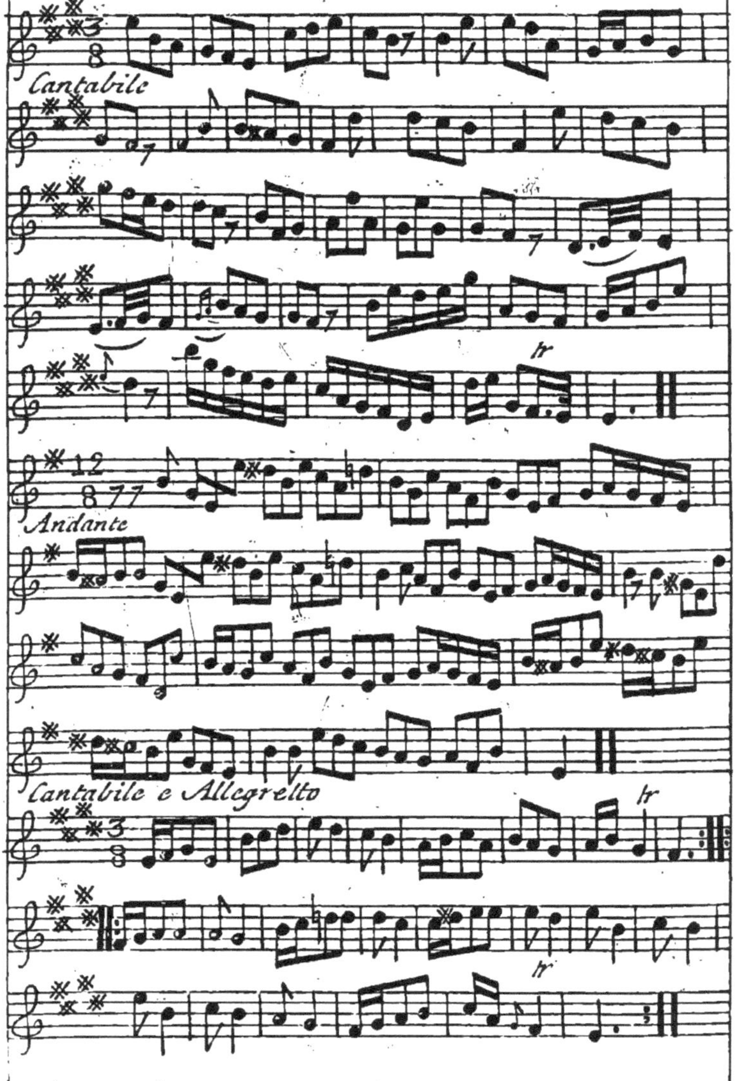

The Prince of Heſſia's March.

Prince of Heſſia's Minuet.

Prince of Orange's March

Vol 2ᵈ Part 5ᵗʰ

D C

10

A Petersburgh favourite Minuet.

The Duke of Brunswick favourite.

Non tujours dire non qui vous rend done.

A famous favourite Minuet.

Hither sweet Ulysses haste By Mr. Arne.

Tempo di Gavotta

Vol 2.d Part 5.th

Prince Charles of Lorain's Minuet.

Prince Maximilian of Hesse's March.

Marshall Saxe's Minuet.

Empress of Russia's favourite Minuet.

Siciliana e dolce.

The Grand Duke of Moscow's Favourite Minuet.

Wap 'em all Wally. or up an war them all Wally.

Wap 'em all Wally. the Irish Way.

D.C.

Prince Charles of Lorain's Favourite Minuet.

Prince Charles of Lorain's March.

Vol 2d Part 5th

Polonese
And.e Larghetto
Polonese
And.e Larghetto
Minuet
1.st
tr
2.d

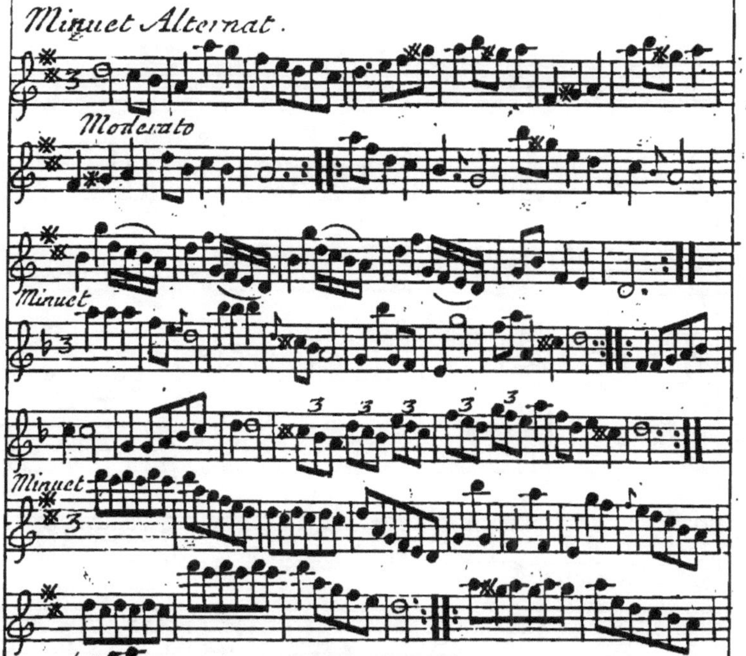
Minuet Alternat.
Moderato
Minuet
Minuet
Minuet.
tr

Andante
Pia
For
Pia
A Favourite Minuet.
Gratioso.
A Favourite Minnet

Polonese

And: Larghetto.

Piа
Minuet

All:

A Portuguese favourite Minuet.

Giga.

Come dear Amanda

22

Why Cloe still these jealous Heats. By Mr. Arne.

Amoroso

Minuet by Mr. Petzold.

Come Myra, Idol of the Swains. By Mr. Arne.

Allegrissimo

Minuet

Minuet Alternat.

End with the first Minuet.

A Hessian Minuet.

Murky

Princess of Orange's favourite Minuet.

Gavott

Vol 2^d Part 5th   End with the Minuet.

A *Portuguese favourite*.

A Berlin favourite Minuet.

Vol 2.ᵈ Part 5.ᵗʰ

Lovely Nancy.

Andante

Gavott

Minuet.

Sonata Allo.

Sonata

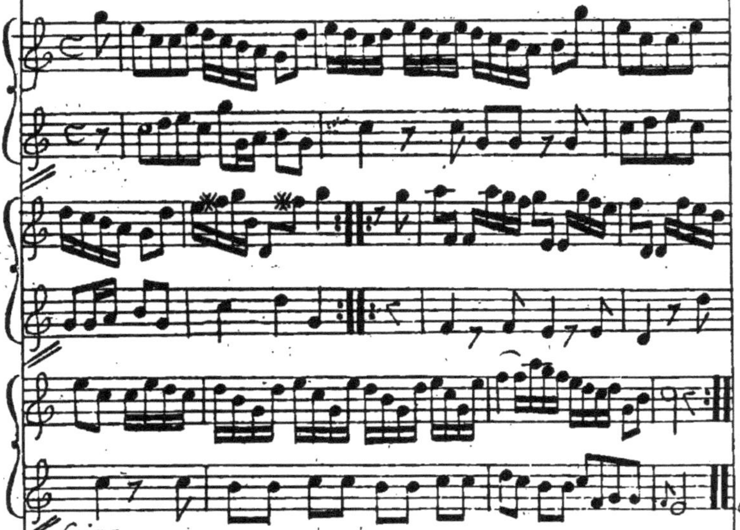

Giga

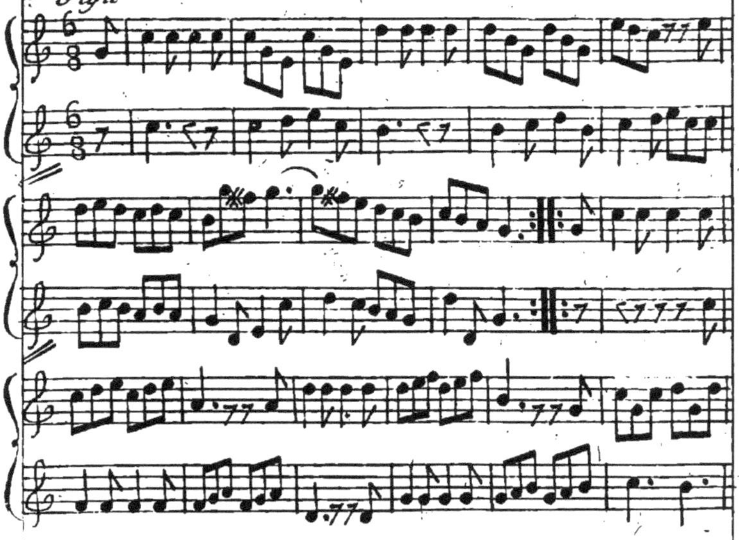

Minuet

Sonata Allº

Sonata

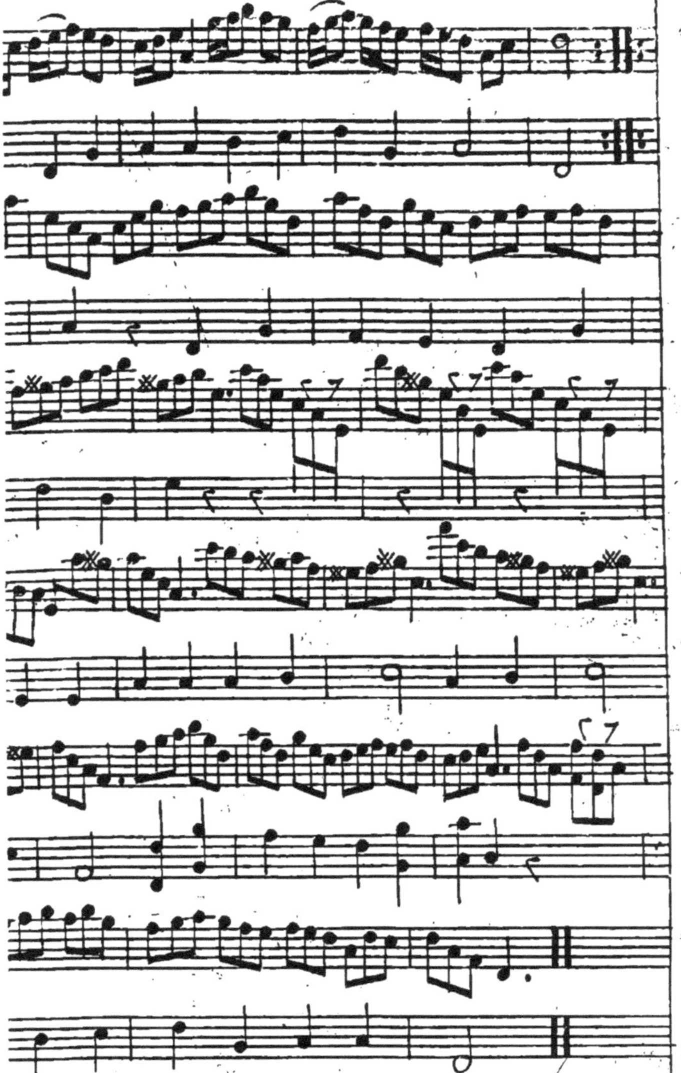

Sonatina
Aria Larghetto
Pia
Minuet alternat.
Pia For
Pia For
2.d Minuet Pia
End with the first Minuet.

Sonatina. In vain you toll.
Largo
Minuet by Mr. Petsold.
Gratioso et alternat:
2.d Minuet by Mr. Petsold.
Amorose
1.st Minuet
Da Capo

Aria

Amoroso

Minuet by Mr. Petzold.

Larghetto

Sonatina. Of ev'ry Sweet.

And.º amoroso

Minuet alternat.
Pia
For
Pia
For
Minuet
tr
Amoroso
tr
End with the first Minuet
A favourite Gavot
Allegro

Minuet.
Sonatina. When Orpheus sweetly.
Andte Largo
Al Tempo di Gavotta. By Mr Petzold.
Moderato

6

Minuet alternat By M.ʳ Petzold.

Larghetto amoroso

2.ᵈ Minuet by M.ʳ Petzold.

Larghetto

End with the
first Minuet

Sonatina Gavotta

Moderato

Giga

Sonatina

Slow

Vol 2.d Part 6.th

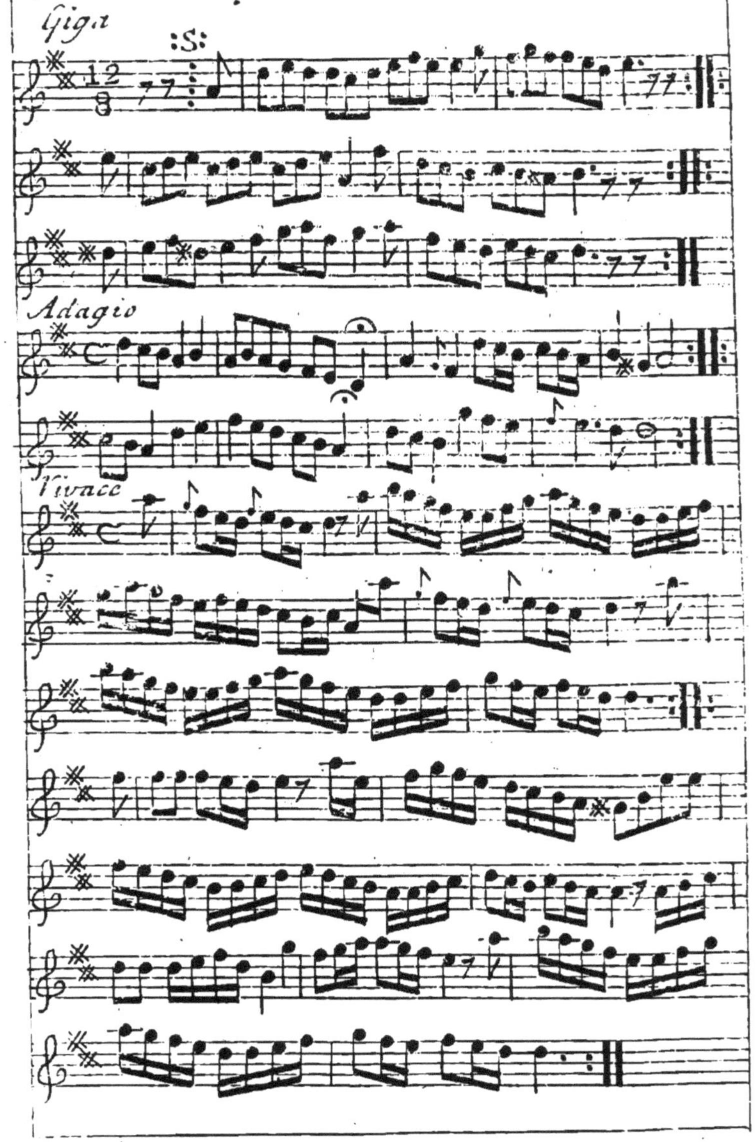
Giga
Adagio
Vivace

Minuet
Paisane
A Dutch Bouren Dance.
D.C.
Paisane.
A Dutch Country Dance.

10
Sonatina

Andante

Vivace

Dolce

Poco All?

End with the Vivace

Sonatina.

Gavotta Rondeau.

Minuet

12
March.

Vivace

Minuet alternat-

Minuet Trio.
Sonatina. Gavotta.
First Minuet D. C.
Minuet.
Harlequinate.
Vol 2d Part 6th

The grand Duke of Moscow's favourite Solo.

Polonese

For

Pia

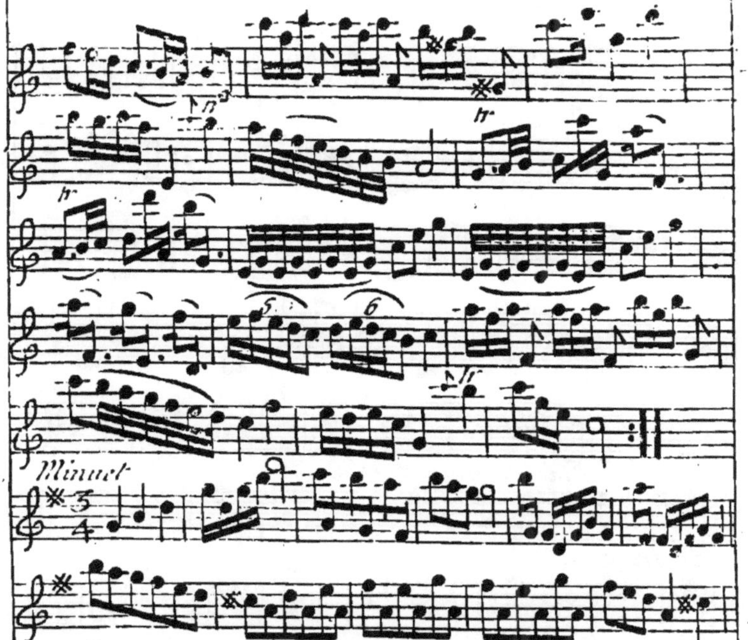
Minuet

16
Ariel's Song.
Andᵗᵉ

Where the Bee sucks.

To fair Fidele's grassy Tomb.

Amoroso.

Minuet by Mʳ. Petzold.

Minuet by Mr. Petzold.

17

18
Sonatina.

The Prince of Orange's March

D.C.

French Horn Duett

Pia

Bourec

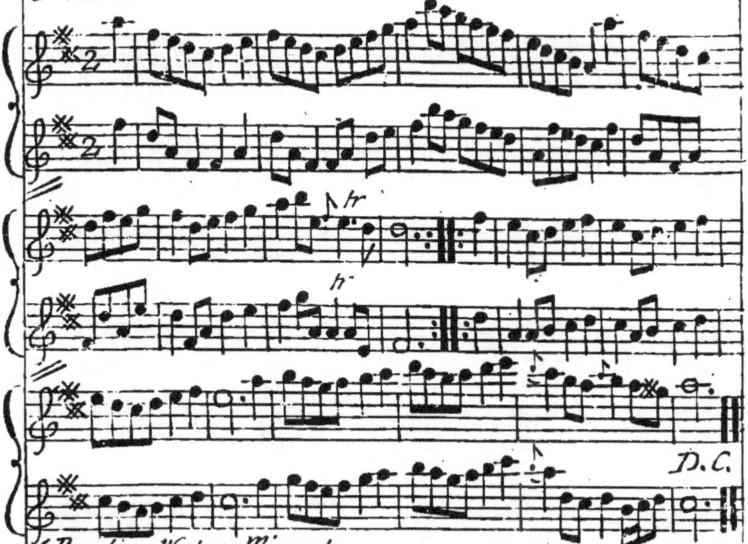

Be:lin Wa'er Minuet

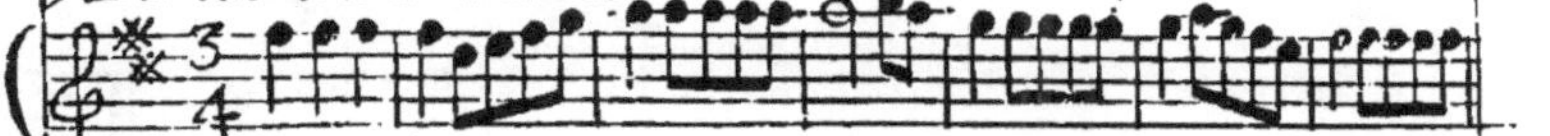

204

Sonatina.

The Seators March.

Gavott Allo.

D C

Minuet

Sonatina. March

Vivace e Pomposo

Vol 2.ᵈ Part 6ᵗʰ   Volti.

Minuet

Minuet

Or Jigg ad Libitum

End with the foregoing Minuet.

24.
Sonatina

Arietta

Symphonia.

Allo

Solo

Volti

Vol 2.d Part 6.th

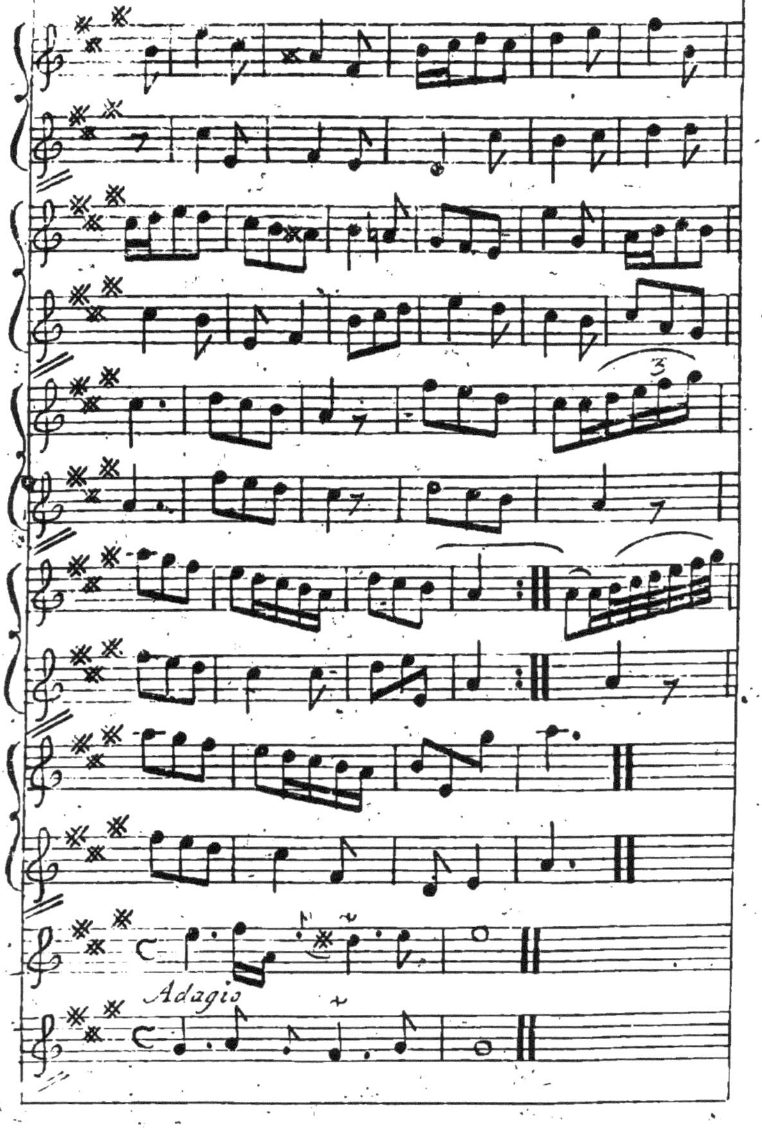
Adagio

Andante

Sonatina   Un jour le grand Collecteur.

Minuet Larghetto.

By the side of a Grove.

Still to be neat.

Sonatina   Bachus C'ost toy que je chante.

Chers amis chantés ma Victoire.

2.ᵈ Rondeau.

The first again and end with the same.

Ye Medley of Mortals.

Sonatina Did you see e'er a Shepherd.

You tell me I'm handsome

Vol 2.d Part 6.th

Allo Moderato

www.ingramcontent.com/pod-product-compliance
Lightning Source LLC
Chambersburg PA
CBHW030820270326
41928CB00007B/814